THE

CHINESE EMPIRE

ILLUSTRATED

THE

CHINESE EMPIRE

ILLUSTRATED:

BEING A SERIES OF VIEWS FROM ORIGINAL SKETCHES,

DISPLAYING

The Scenery, Architecture, Social Habits, &c.,

OF THAT ANCIENT AND EXCLUSIVE NATION,

BY THOMAS ALLOM, ESQ.

WITH

HISTORICAL AND DESCRIPTIVE LETTERPRESS,

BY THE REV G. N. WRIGHT, M.A.

ADAPTED AND ABRIDGED BY
D.J.M. TATE

JOHN NICHOLSON LTD.
HONG KONG

First published 1988
Second impression 1989
by John Nicholson Ltd.
23rd Floor, Unit D, United Centre,
95 Queensway,
GPO Box 11204, Hong Kong

ISBN 962 328 002 5

The Publisher and compiler would like to thank Mr. Michael Sweet of
Antiques of the Orient, Singapore for his help in preparing this book.

Designed by T & Y Design Associates, Malaysia.
Printed in Malaysia by Art Printing Works Sdn. Bhd.
Published by John Nicholson Ltd.,
23rd floor, United Centre, 95 Queensway, Hong Kong.

Contents

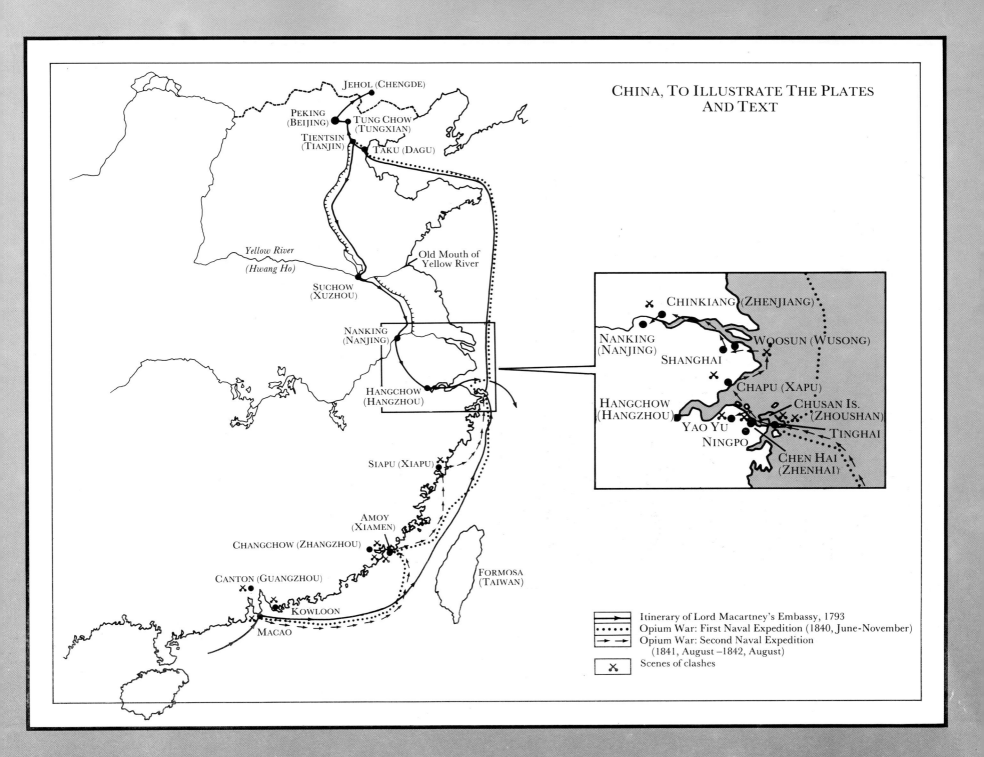

CHINA, TO ILLUSTRATE THE PLATES
AND TEXT

JEHOL (CHENGDE)

PEKING
(BEIJING)
TUNG CHOW
(TUNGXIAN)
TIENTSIN
(TIANJIN)
TAKU (DAGU)

Yellow River
(Hwang Ho)

Old Mouth of
Yellow River

SUCHOW
(XUZHOU)

NANKING
(NANJING)

HANGCHOW
(HANGZHOU)

SIAPU (XIAPU)

AMOY
(XIAMEN)

CHANGCHOW (ZHANGZHOU)

CANTON (GUANGZHOU)

KOWLOON

MACAO

FORMOSA
(TAIWAN)

CHINKIANG (ZHENJIANG)

NANKING
(NANJING)
SHANGHAI

WOOSUN (WUSONG)

CHAPU (XAPU)

CHUSAN IS.
(ZHOUSHAN)

HANGCHOW
(HANGZHOU)

YAO YU
NINGPO

TINGHAI

CHEN HAI
(ZHENHAI)

Itinerary of Lord Macartney's Embassy, 1793
Opium War: First Naval Expedition (1840, June–November)
Opium War: Second Naval Expedition
   (1841, August –1842, August)

✗   Scenes of clashes

Introduction

Drawn by T.Allom.   Engraved by W. Floyd.

THE sixty fine engravings of China which constitute the basis of this book have been selected from the one hundred and forty-three plates which comprise Allom and Wright's *The Chinese Empire Illustrated*, 'being a series of views from original sketches, displaying The Scenery, Architecture, Social Habits, etc. of that ancient and exclusive nation ... with historical and descriptive letterpress' — a monumental work with a monumental title which appeared in its final edition in 1859, the original volumes having been published just after the close of the First Opium War sixteen years earlier. Apart from their intrinsic interest, Allom's drawings stand out as works of art in their own right, for Allom was an exceptionally good draughtsman and architect, while the accompanying 'historical and descriptive letterpress' by the Revd. G.N. Wright, a pioneer Protestant missionary in China, provides both information and entertainment.

The occasion for the publication of their work was the collision between Britain and China that took the form of the so-called Opium Wars of 1839–42 and 1856–60. In fact, their material is centred on the first of these two wars. The outbreak of the second war merely inspired the final version of 1859 (by a different publisher) which only differed from its predecessor in the rearrangement of the order of the plates (twenty-five new plates, most of which are not of China at all, being added) and by including an update of recent events in China, a detailed description of 'the way thither', and a brief résumé of China's history.

With its publication, Allom and Wright provided the most comprehensive view of China which had ever been made available to the general reader in the West. However, the China Allom's drawings portrayed was the China of the early part, rather than the middle, of the nineteenth century, for apparently Allom himself had never been there. His drawings and sketches are based on the drawings and sketches of others. One of his main sources was the work of William Alexander, a young artist who accompanied Lord Macartney's famous embassy to the Chinese Court in 1793. Alexander sketched copiously and well on that mission, and the fruits of his labours appeared in various publications including Sir George Staunton's *An Historical Account of the Embassy to China* (1797) and his own *The Costume of China* (1805) and *Picturesque Representations of the Dress and Manners of the Chinese* (1814). For scenes related to the war itself, Allom relied mainly on the sketches produced by two participants in it — Captain Stoddart, R.N., and Lieutenant White of the Royal Marines. While the source of the Stoddart and White sketches is generally acknowledged, those adapted from Alexander invariably are not.

The selection of plates presented in the present volume consists of a representative cross-section of the engravings from the original work. Covering a wide spectrum of Chinese life, they have been regrouped by theme in place of the somewhat haphazard arrangement in which they first appeared. While the illustrations themselves are very largely self-explanatory, the narrative — suitably abridged and adapted so as to be digestible to a twentieth century audience — gives depth and insight. Terms and allusions which may require elucidation have been done so in brief footnotes, and a guide to the spelling of names of principal places mentioned in the text may be found in the glossary at the end of this book. The only section which might appear to be a little less than self-explanatory is the last one which is entitled 'China at War'. For although Allom and Wright's production was inspired by the First Opium War, and the scenes in it are held together by the thread of circumstance provided by British military operations, the authors were not interested in making a war book but in revealing the nature of the country with which Britain was at war. The illustrations of actual military engagements and clashes are therefore episodic, and as will soon be noted, the action of marines storming beaches or of soldiers enfilading beneath the walls of ancient Chinese cities get absorbed — after a true Chinese tradition — in the picturesque backdrop of mountains, bridges and pagodas. Wright did indeed provide an outline of the main course of the war, which is too long and tedious to reproduce here; for the reader who wants to know about the sequence of events and the location of the campaigns, the map provided at the beginning of this book and the account provided in the section 'China at War' should suffice. In other words the justification for republishing — in a condensed form — this nineteenth century masterpiece lies first and foremost in the artistry of the illustrations. From the historical point of view they should serve as an appetizer, leading the reader to want to know more. It should also be remembered, however, that when Allom's pictures first appeared, they were unveiling the mysteries of that 'ancient and exclusive nation' to the outside world; today this selective reproduction preserves for us sights which no longer exist.

The transliteration of Chinese names and terms tends to be a source of unending confusion. In this volume the idiosyncratic spelling and punctuation of Allom and Wright has been retained in the main text, while the more familiar Wade-Giles system has, in most instances, been used in the commentaries and notes, although personal and place names occasionally follow the form most commonly found in books in English on China. As the reader will already know, modern Chinese spelling in English is different again, and follows the official *pinyin* style. For this the reader is referred to the Glossary at the end of this book.

D.J.M. TATE
Kuala Lumpur
October 1987

I
IMPERIAL
CHINA

The following selection of plates on 'Imperial China' affords glimpses of the traditional Chinese establishment. Despite the condescending tone of the descriptions which accompany the illustrations, an impression is conveyed of the presence of a highly sophisticated culture which was very different from, but by no means inferior to, that of the West. Until the Chinese door was prised open by force, very few Westerners had obtained access to the sanctums of Chinese power. The Jesuits had done so in the seventeeth century; in their attempt to convert China to Christianity, but after their eclipse, Western glimpses behind the Chinese screen were limited to the occasional visits of travellers or ambassadors. Lord Macartney was one of these ambassadors, and his embassy of the 1790s provided a considerable amount of the material from which Allom drew his pictures.

From the confines of their factories at Canton, the Europeans could grasp a measure of the Chinese scene, but the south of China was not the north, and the essence of Chinese authority resided at Peking. That authority was concentrated in the person of the Emperor who was absolute to a degree that no Western ruler ever attained. Not only was he the titular head of every aspect of Chinese life and affairs, but he also played a direct and personal role. He was his own Prime Minister, presiding over meetings with his officials, personally scrutinizing petitions from the provinces, making laws and issuing decrees, deciding on judicial sentences, making appointments and dismissals, giving his personal assent to treaties, even selecting the best candidates in the civil service examinations. He was supported by a well-organized and intricate bureaucracy manned by an elite civil service moulded in the precepts of Confucius. His provincial governors were directly answer-able to him and a skilful system of checks and balances prevented the rise of overmighty subjects. The only constraint on imperial power was the need to conform to the Confucian ethic.

This imperial system, honed into perfection over the course of two thousand years, reached its apogee under the Ch'ing (Qing) dynasty. However, the Ch'ing emperors were not ethnic Chinese at all, but Manchu Tartars, a nomadic race whose home was the Manchurian steppes and who had conquered China in 1644 at the expense of the native Ming emperors. The Chinese of the nineteenth century were therefore a subject people. But the subjects had overcome their masters, for the Manchus had found it necessary to adopt and assimilate to Chinese ways in order to maintain their power. In fact the government of nineteenth century China was a kind of dyarchy, power being shared by Manchu and Chinese officials. But the Manchus had the last word.

It was this superiority of Chinese culture and civilization which had developed in isolation from the other main centres of civilization on earth that gave the Chinese their self-centred view of the world. Theirs was the 'Middle Kingdom', the fount of culture. Other states and other people who lived beyond its pale could only be less civilized and inferior. Like the Greeks, the Chinese regarded those who did not know or follow their values as barbarians who, if they approached Chinese shores, could only come and be treated as bearers of tribute. This concept of the universe, the static nature of Chinese society, and the influence of the conservative philosophy of Confucianism ill-prepared the Chinese to cope with the challenge of the new industrial civilization of the West when it irrupted into their world in the nineteenth century.

1
The Po-To-La
or Great Temple
near Jehol,
Tartary

The Great Temple built by the K'ang-hsi (Kangxi) Emperor at Jehol a former summer residence of the Manchu rulers. It was modelled after the Potala at Lhasa in Tibet and was known as the Putuo Zong-sheng Temple. As intimated in the Introduction, this engraving is based on an Allom drawing copied from one by William Alexander.

2
Gardens of the Imperial Palace, Peking

THERE are two distinct cities within the walls of Peking, one occupied by Chinese, the other by Tartars exclusively.[1] In the latter of these are the chief public offices, several sacred institutes, colleges, halls, and, lastly, in the very centre of this labyrinth, the imperial palace and gardens. Three spacious gates pierce the imperial wall, opening communication with the external or Chinese city, which is also fenced and fortified; and an inner enclosure, called "the prohibited wall," surrounds an area of about two square miles, devoted entirely to the imperial household, and only entered by his majesty's retinue or his visitors. The mural defences of the palace are built of bright red varnished bricks, covered with shining yellow tiles, whence they are also styled "The Yellow Wall," and are upwards of twenty feet in height. The inner surface of the enclosure is varied by the construction of artificial mountains, the excavation of lakes with little islands floating on their tranquil bosoms, and running rivulets, interrupted occasionally by picturesque cataracts; summer-houses and pavilions adorn the margin of the waters, and impart an interest to the numerous islands; and the grouping of fanciful edifices, with clusters of trees, and masses of rock-work, necessarily produce a most agreeable illusion with respect to both distance and magnitude. One great reservoir, or lake, supplies the minor basins within the gardens, and its surface is constantly animated by the arrival and departure of pleasure-junks and barges belonging to the attendants and retainers of the palace.

Pleasure appears to reign supremely in these fairy lands, but the double walls, that prohibit surprise, are not unnecessary, nor has the imperial throne been always "a bed of roses." There is a perilous uncertainty attendant upon making rice the national food; and even the emperor's palace was not safe from the violence of the hungry, in those days of famine that periodically visit his dominions. The markets of Peking are frequently plundered in the most daring manner, and all the courage of the emperor's tiger-hearted guards is required to protect the Tartarian city from assault. Nor are these the only dangers to which the imperial person is exposed. Though the succession to the throne depends on the arbitrary nomination of the reigning prince, this arrangement does not always prevent usurpations.

On the summit of the loftiest eminence in the accompanying illustration,[2] stands a monument of singular structure, but of still more singular history; it marks the death place of the last of those emperors who had beautified the whole of these enchanting grounds, and raised so many gorgeous buildings amidst their scenery. A man[3] whom fortune seemed to favour availed himself of the weakness and the luxury of the court; with an army of Chinese, first collected under the hope of bringing about better times, and kept together afterwards by the tempting bait of plunder, he marched to the gates of Peking. The ill-fated monarch,[4] too slightly supported, and possessed of too little energy to repel, determined to save his offspring from the danger of dishonour, stabbed his only daughter, and then hung himself from a tree in the enclosure.

---

[1] *The Tartar City was founded by the Mongol emperor, Khublai (Kublai) Khan, and restored by the Ming Emperor, Yung-lo (Yongle).*

[2] *Prospect or Coal Hill, an artificial mound sited just north of the Forbidden City in the heart of the Tartar City.*

[3] *The Chinese rebel, Li Tzu-cheng, whose capture of Peking caused the collapse of the Ming dynasty, a result which turned out to the benefit of the invading Manchus and not to the rebel General.*

[4] *The Ch'ung-chen (Chungzhen) Emperor, the last Ming ruler.*

3
The Emperor Taou-kwang Reviewing his Guards, Palace of Peking

IN the court of the Three Halls, in the palace at Peking, an annual review of the Tartar guards is held, by the emperor in person, as the new year opens. Along the terrace in front of the extended colonnades, the great officers of the palace are ranged; while Taou-kwang,[1] seated on the throne, and surrounded by his ministers, looks complacently down upon the brave defenders of the yellow standard.[2]

These Tartar lifeguards might possibly display the most courageous bearing, if called to defend their monarch's crown; but, their mode of life, and poor discipline, do not afford much favourable promise. Although it is a practice of the Ping-poo,[3] a military tribunal, to institute comparisons between their great officers, and the most ferocious kinds of animals; recommending that they should be "tigers in their fierce deportment;" although they deck their troops with skins of the lion and the tiger, and paint their shields with the most hideous devices; yet their uniform is a mere theatrical costume, and their discipline a most entire mockery of the military art.

The full uniform of a Tartar officer on a field-day, or occasion of review, is complicated and costly, but not compact. A polished helmet, resembling an inverted cone, and ending in a crest about eight inches above the head, is adorned with gold and with coloured hair; a robe of blue or purple silk, and studded with gilt buttons, envelopes the person, and descends to the boots, which are of black satin; while the handles of their swords and horns of their bows, and stocks of their match-locks glitter with precious gems. The dress of the privates is less gorgeous, but equally fantastic; their robes are of stuff striped in imitation of tiger-skin, their cap or helmet lofty, and shaped as a tiger's head; and, on their round shields of bamboo cane are raised devices, either a dragon's figure, or a tiger's head. No duty, however, seems to be imposed on the imperial guard, beyond the watchful care of their august master; they are permitted to pursue commercial avocations, relieving each other in their duty at the palace; but they reside always within the Tartar city, which is distinct, and separated by a lofty wall from the Chinese section of Peking. The ceremony of a review within the Imperial palace is necessarily imposing; the costume, if not suited to European taste, is still rich and brilliant; the banners are always numerous and of the most gaudy colours, while palanquins, lanterns, dragons, and other devices, carried by the standard-bearers, confer a character of sumptuousness, in which the Chinese imagine that true nobility consists. None but the imperial band is allowed to perform: it includes kettle-drums and gongs of large diameter, wind instruments shaped like dragons, serpents, and fish, besides an unlimited number of clarionets and lutes.

---

[1] *Hsüan-tsung (Xuanzong), the Tao-kuang (Daoguang) Emperor, the eighth of the Ch'ing dynasty,.who reigned from 1820 to 1850.*

[2] *The Tartar Guards, comprising the bannermen, were a hereditary body descended from the soldiers who had taken part in the Manchu conquest of China. They provided the guard for the imperial palaces, the principal cities and other strategic points.*

[3] *Ping-poo (Bingbu), or Board of War, one of the six boards or ministries of the Imperial Government, which had the functions of a Ministry of Defence.*

4
Hall of Audience, Palace of Yuen-min-Yuen[1] Peking

A noble park, improperly called the Gardens of Yuen-min-Yuen, is situated about three leagues[2] north-west of Peking, and occupies an area of eleven square miles. Here are no less than *thirty* distinct imperial residences, each surrounded with all the necessary buildings for lodging the numerous state officers, servants, and artificers, that are required, not only on occasions of court and public days, but for the regular conduct of the household. Each of these assemblages includes so great a number of separate structures, that at a little distance the appearance is precisely that of a comfortable village, and of tolerable extent.

Amongst these thirty groups of painted palaces, the Hall of Audience is the most conspicuous for its magnitude, ornament and proportions. Elevated on a platform of granite, about four feet above the surrounding level, an oblong structure stands, one hundred and twenty feet in length, forty-five in breadth, and in height twenty. A row of large wooden columns surrounds the hall and supports a heavy projecting roof; while an inner tier, of less substantial pillars, marks the area of the chambers: the intervals of the latter, being filled with brick-work to the height of four feet, form the enclosing screen or walls of the chief apartment. Above these the space is occupied with lattice work, covered with oiled paper, and capable of being thrown open, when the temperature of the hall demands it. On the ceiling are described squares, circles, polygons, and other mathematical figures, in various combinations, and charged with endless shades of gaudy colours. The floor is a more chaste piece of workmanship, consisting of slabs of a beautiful grey marble, disposed chequer-wise, and with the most accurate and perfect precision in the jointing. In a recess at the centre of one end stands the imperial throne, composed entirely of cedar richly and delicately carved, the canopy being supported by wooden pillars painted with red, green, and blue colours. Two large brass kettle-drums, occasionally planted before the door, and there beaten on the approach of the emperor, form part of the furniture of the hall, the rest consisting of Chinese paintings, an English chiming-clock, made by Clarke of Leadenhall-street,[3] and a pair of circular fans formed of the wings of the argus-pheasant, and mounted on polished ebony poles. These stand on each side of the throne, above which are inscribed, in the Chinese letter and language, "True, great, refulgent, splendid," and beneath these pompous words, the much more pithy one — *"Happiness."*

The columns in all cases — within the hall, beneath the imperial canopy, and those that sustain the overhanging roof — are without capitals; and the only substitute for an architrave[4] is the bressumer, or horizontal beam on which the projecting rafters of the roof recline. Below this architrave and between the columns, wooden screens are interposed, painted with the most glaring hues of the brightest colours, profusely intermixed with gilding. Over the whole of this fancy-work a net of gilded wire is stretched, to protect it against the invasion of swallows, and other enemies to the eaves and the cornices of buildings.

---

[1]*Better known as the Old Summer Palace, built as a summer residence by the K'ang-hsi Emperor, and looted and destroyed by British and French troops when they occupied Peking in 1860. It was used for the reception of foreign missions.*

[2]*About 8 miles.*

[3]*Leadenhall Street, one of the principal streets of the City of London.*

[4]*Architrave: an architectural term for the bottom supporting beam of the entablature (the uppermost part) of a classical building.*

5
The Imperial Travelling-Palace at the Hoo-kew-shan

NO private palace of his humiliated mandarins,[1] no public inn of his enslaved subjects, is ever honoured by the imperial presence; when the court makes a tour of pleasure or policy, the retinue is lodged at "travelling palaces" erected for their reception. These occur along the great high-roads that connect the principal cities of the empire, and some of them exceed in sumptuousness, all in picturesque surroundings, the much-celebrated palace and gardens of Pe-king.

Keang-nan[2] is a fair and a fertile province, enjoying variety of seasons, of soil, of scenery. In this province, in the midst of happy faces, and amongst sunny hills, is the imperial travelling palace of the Hoo-kew-shan or Tiger Mound. The locality is about nine le[3] north-west of Soo-chow-foo,[4] the second city of the first rank in the province, and is one of the most famed in Chinese story, for its romantic scenery, its commanding prospects, and its ancient legends. From the conspicuousness of the mound that rises so precipitously from the level country, and which has now become a valuable landmark to the mariner, this "gathering of rocky eminences" is also known as the Hae-yung-fung, "or sea-rising peak." Antique relics of various descriptions lend an interest to this remarkable locality.

The summit of the bold rock that rises abruptly behind the imperial buildings, and is connected with the opposite cliffs by an arched viaduct spanning a deep ravine, is surmounted by the beautiful Han-meaou pagoda of seven stories. From this graceful structure, formerly attached to the Ho-tsing temple, the prospect is extensive and delightful, forming, from the earliest periods of native landscapes a subject of the most enthusiastic admiration. In the centre of the accompanying view may be observed an upright stone inscribed with the words "How-kew," the name of the place.

This assemblage of ancient remains, this group of picturesque hills, rendered interesting by so many associations, is now included within the grounds and the gardens of an imperial palace.

[1]*For definition of 'mandarin', see the following narrative on page 11.*

[2]*Kiangnan was under the control of a* tsung-tu (zongdu) *or Governor-General, but because of its great size was subdivided by the Emperor K'ang-hsi (1661–1722) into the provinces of Kiangsu and Anhwei, each under its own governor (fu-yuan). However, the post of Governor-General was retained.*

[3]*Le* (li), *'the Chinese mile', approximately one-third of an English mile, although this varied from place to place.*

[4]*Süchow is situated in Kiangsu, one of the most thickly-populated regions of China, and was famed for its beauty and as a centre for scholarship.*

6
A Mandarin Paying a Visit of Ceremony

IMITATING their emperor, the mandarins[1] of China adopt the palanquin form of vehicle, and the circumstances accompanying their visits of ceremony, although they include many that are common to the aristocracy of Great Britain, are nevertheless extraordinary and characteristic. The chair is generally open, but furnished with curtains and tassels of silk; and a silken net-work, often interlaced with silver thread, covers the convex roof, which is surmounted by a ball or a button. The extremities of two long bamboo poles, which pass through staples in the sides of the sedan, are connected by cords, through the bend or curve of which a short piece of bamboo is passed, the ends resting on the shoulders of the chairmen, thus dividing the whole weight equally between the four carriers. For the sake both of speed and splendour, four others are always ready to succeed to the labour, when the first four shall exhibit the least symptoms of fatigue.

Before the sedan-chair a crowd of servants advance, some beating gongs, others extolling in loud tones the virtues of their master, and calling upon the worthless rabble to make way for the approaching cortège: besides whom a number of umbrella-carriers and chain-bearers, distinguished by caps of wire with a feather in the top, often attend such processions, to terrify the ignorant and enslaved spectators, who are peremptorily desired to stand and stare; and, lastly, as no public ceremony of joy or sorrow in China, is complete without the introduction of the bamboo, a posse of fellows, in the pay of the great man, also attend his progress, armed with strong pieces of the national cane, to belabour any unhappy obstructors who endeavour

to obtain a peep at the petty tyrant as he passes. The cortege having arrived at its destination, the gate of some mandarin who is to be honoured by a visit, the conductor advances, and, presenting a long jointed tablet, coloured red, and illuminated richly — unless the family are in mourning, when the tablet is white and the letters blue — displaying the rank and title of his master, he mentions the purport of his coming. This placard, like the rent-roll of our country squires, obtains a degree of respect exactly proportioned to its contents. Should the title be eminent, the host comes to the gate, and even outside, to receive his visitor; should it be otherwise, more reserve, or less enthusiasm, is shown accordingly.

The mode of recognition here amongst acquaintances is extremely courteous; joining their clenched hands — a plan which is often preferable to the application of the open palm — they raise them afterwards to the forehead, at the same time addressing the customary inquiry after the health of each other; and, amongst those who are considered the most refined and most perfect masters of politeness, genuflexions are not uncommon. Upon the termination of the visit, and return of the visitor to his sedan, the same ceremonies are repeated, some of them of course in an inverted order.

---

[1] *The term 'mandarin', derived from the Portuguese word* mandar, *to command, was used by Westerners to denote the highest class of executive officials in Manchu China, called* kuan. *The* kuan *were divided into nine grades, each grade being indicated by a coloured button worn on the official's dress.*

II
CITIES OF
CHINA

The cities of China presented another aspect of that ancient civilization and culture which was exposed in detail to Western eyes only after the Opium War. Many were of very ancient foundation, far predating the average European city, and contained within their walls buildings of great age, beauty and rich historical association. Virtually every Chinese city was walled, the extent of the walls and their size being a reflection of their status. For the Chinese city was by definition a centre of administration and was classified into one of three grades denoting whether it was a provincial, prefectorial or district capital. The walls of a Chinese city could be extensive; those of Peking (including the Tartar and Chinese cities) had a circumference of twenty miles, those of Nanking, twenty-six. Not all the land inside the walls was built upon; there were market gardens, temple precincts and private parks attached to the residences of the upper classes. Other features of any Chinese city were its temple of Confucius, and the temple to its own particular city

deity. Pagodas provided another feature; originally designed as shrines for relics of the Buddha, they came to be regarded as an essential element in promoting harmony with the forces of nature (the feng-shui), and their presence an ineffable influence for the welfare of the locality they were situated in.

The handful of Chinese cities portrayed here are of course those of easy access to Westerners, primarily centres of trade along the coast, or places on the route to Peking. Macao is the oldest European settlement in China, having been officially leased to the Portuguese in 1557 against a nominal annual rent, but the Portuguese did not succeed in shaking off token Chinese sovereignty till 1887. Canton was the port best known to Westerners prior to the Opium War since it was there that they were eventually forced to confine their trade with China. But even so, very few Westerners ever penetrated the city proper; they were confined to some 21 acres outside the city walls on the island of Shameen, fronting the Pearl River where — on land rented from the Co-hong — they were permitted to erect their 'factories' — that is, places of residence, offices and warehouses. Amoy and Ningpo were other ports which had been known to the European traders; Ningpo was one of the earliest Portuguese settlements, while the English tried to open up trade at both Ningpo and Amoy. The other cities shown, including the great centres of Nanking and Peking, were only opened to Western eyes during the course of the Opium War. Hong Kong was a different case. It was a new city, the child of war. It sprang up in the years which followed as a monument to the beneficial effects of combined Western and Chinese enterprise, technically a foreign city but with Chinese roots.

7
Facade of the
Great Temple,
Macao

SO slight is Portuguese tenure or title at Macao, that the Chinese maintain here, in neighbourship with this despised race of foreigners, one of the most remarkable, most venerated, and really graceful buildings in the empire, dedicated to the worship of Fo.[1] The architecture is more intelligible as a design, more perfect in execution, and less grotesque, than the majority of Buddhist temples; the situation on the water-side, amidst forest-trees and natural rock, is inconceivably beautiful; and the mode in which the architects have made use of all these accessories to grace and harmony is highly meritorious.

The Neang-mako or Old Temple of the Lady, is situated about half a mile from the city of Macao, in a north-west direction; and the walk thither, although obstructed by the usual inconveniences of Chinese roads, is rendered specially agreeable by the prospects it commands, along its whole length, of the inner port, and of the green hills of Lapa.[2] From its sunk, and shaded site, the temple is not seen until the visitor comes suddenly upon the steep rocky steps that descend to the spacious esplanade before it. Two tall red flag-staffs, however, in front of the temple, make a conspicuous mark for those acquainted with the locality; being conspicuous at all hours, by the three golden balls that surmount them, by the square frame-work that is attached to them, and by the imperial standard that adorns them. At the foot of the broad stairs are three great monumental stones, closely inscribed with names, titles, eulogies and other mementos. Beyond these commemorative pillars, is the wide, open, agreeable esplanade, represented in the illustration; on one side of which is part of the facade of the building, on the other the estuary or inlet, into which the Peninsula of Macao projects. The scene in front composed of religious devotees, venders of various commodities, jugglers, ballad singers, sailors, soldiers, mandarins, and beggars, is common to all the sea-ports of China.

[1]*Buddha*

[2]*Lapa, an island on the mainland side of Macao.*

8
The Pria Granda, Macao

This particular view no longer exists, half the crescent having been absorbed by reclamation. It is based on a sketch by Warner Varnham, an English tea inspector at Canton who was also a pupil of the well-known painter, George Chinnery, who resided in Macao for many years and is buried there.

MACAO, where once a flourishing trade existed, where Spain, Portugal's haughty neighbour, was compelled to strike her own flag, and hoist the standard of her rival, whenever she approached the shores of China — whenever English enterprise found a profitable field for operation — this Macao is now simply, solely, a record of the past.

The Pria, or Praya Granda,[1] is the most flattering surviving specimen of this emporium of Oriental trade. Approached from the water, this fine promenade presents a striking and agreeable appearance. A row of handsome houses, extending along the beach for upwards of seven hundred yards, is built in a crescent form, in obedience to the graceful and regular bend of the bay. In front, a spacious walk is formed, on an artificial embankment faced with stone, interrupted, occasionally, by jetties for landing goods, and by steps for descending to the water. Here is the residence of the Portuguese governor, and here also is the English factory, plain substantial buildings; besides the Custom-house, distinguished by the display of the Imperial flag in front. At the termination of what is called the High-street, stands the Senate House, a structure whose pretensions to architectural beauty are of the humblest character, but its dimensions considerable. Beyond the Praya Granda, a mixed assemblage of styles presents itself, including English houses, towers of Portuguese churches, Chinese temples, and domestic roofs, generally grotesque. The church of St. Joseph, the most spacious and beautiful of the twelve which the first settlers raised here, dedicated to the Apostles, is a college, and richly decorated. The sea-view of the city does not partake of the Chinese character, because those natives who reside at Macao inhabit the back streets only, and their dwellings being but one story in height, are concealed by the Portuguese and English houses that surround them: the Chinese are generally dealers in grain, vegetables, and sea-stores, in addition to their employments of joiners, smiths, tailors, &c.

Besides the college of St. Joseph, Macao boasts a grammar-school of royal foundation, and some few other institutions of Portuguese origin devoted to literature; amongst the charitable establishments is an asylum for female orphans. At the extremity of the Praya Granda is a spacious and elegant demesne called the *Casa,* in which is ostentatiously shown a natural grotto, where Camoens, once the Portuguese judge at Macao, is said to have written the greater part of his Lusiad.[2]

The dulness of Macao is unbroken by any incidents of interest, if we exempt the annual immigration of Cantonese families, during the sultry season in the great city, of which the Portuguese avail themselves by holding a grand carnival. This feast is celebrated with the utmost costliness and enthusiasm — balls, masques, concerts, spectacles, and all other amusements, that minister to the pleasure of soft, southern Europe, are called in, to aid in giving effect to the Macao carnival.

---

[1]*The Praia Grande, now bisected by a road and a bridge which links Macao with the neighbouring islands of Taipa and Coloane.*

[2]*See p. 55.*

9
Macao, from the Forts of Heang-shan

MACAO occupies a position rather of beauty than strength; for the rocky summits that surround its peninsular site also command it, and the waters that wash its winding base are navigable by vessels of considerable burden. The city stands upon a peninsula, three miles in length by one in breadth, one side of which is curved into a beautiful bay, the opposite being somewhat convex towards the sea; the ridge of this rocky eminence, as well as its sloping sides, being covered with churches, and convents, and turrets, and tall houses, such as are seen in Europe. A narrow sandy isthmus joins the peninsula to the heights of Heang-shan, which are crowned with forts, to awe the humbled settlers; and an embattled wall, after the jealous fashion of the Chinese, crosses the isthmus, and forms an entire separation between its Christian inhabitants and the Chinese. It is said that this barrier was first erected to check the incursions of Roman Catholic priests, who were much addicted to the practice of stealing Chinese children, from a desire to convert them to a saving faith.[1] The end was certainly laudable, but not the means. The rigidity with which the Portuguese are ruled, and the well-known character of the Chinese as individualists would rather induce a belief that the charge of kidnapping was a forgery, invented as a pretext for building up this rampart. A presiding mandarin (Tso-tang) constantly resides in Macao, and gives evidence of the flimsy nature of Portuguese tenure there, by occasionally stopping the supply of provisions intended for the Christians — by enforcing strictly the conditions of their occupancy, such as prohibiting the erection of new houses, or repairs of old ones — and by inspecting the Portuguese forts, to see that no additional strength has been given to them, nor any increase made to the garrison of four hundred men. Without a license, (for which a stipend is expected,) none of these conditions may be violated with impunity; nor can the Portuguese accomplish such objects secretly, all manual labour being exercised exclusively by Chinese residents.

The Portuguese executive at Macao consists of a military governor, a judge, and a bishop, each of whom enjoys a salary of £600 per annum; a sum considerable indeed, when the insignificance of their services is remembered. The Chinese portion of the population, about thirty thousand souls, is subject to native authorities solely; the European, including Portuguese by birth, *Mesticos* — also Portuguese, but descended from Malay mothers — and foreigners of all classes, in all not more than four thousand, is under the nominal rule of the Portuguese governor. This power, however, often proves too weak to compete with the lords of the soil, who occasionally order all foreigners to withdraw upon a few hours' notice, under pain of confiscation of property and loss of liberty; thereby restricting trade — the only occupation which Christian settlers exercise here — so frequently and so much, that the temples of Macao are without worshippers, the dwellings untenanted, the harbour almost forsaken.

---

[1] *The forts and wall across the isthmus were built in 1573 during the reign of the Ming Emperor Wan-li (Wanli), ostensibly to prevent the kidnapping of Chinese coolies but in effect to keep an eye on the Portuguese.*

10
The European
Factories, Canton[1]

ALTHOUGH permitted to establish commercial agents, and erect factories or stores for business, and residence at Canton, all foreigners have hitherto been treated with the utmost illiberality by the Imperial government. Notwithstanding the warmth of the climate, and consequent insalubrity of a residence almost below the sea-level, and surrounded by stagnant water, the site appropriated to the foreign factories of all nations, a space not exceeding eight hundred feet in length or frontage, by four hundred in depth, was formerly a putrid marsh. Piles being driven to a great depth, a secure foundation was obtained, and on these "The Thirteen *Hongs*" have been erected.[2] Flag-staffs in front of each are adorned with their respective national colours, and every factory is designated by some distinguishing or descriptive epithet, after the Chinese custom. The British factory is called "the Hong that ensures tranquillity;" the American, "of the Many Fountains;" the Dutch, "of the Yellow Flag;" the Austrian, of "the Twin-Eagle;" the Swedish, Parsee, Danish, and French, are also similarly designated. At the back of the Factories, is a narrow creek charged with all the impurities from the city-sewers; and in front are stairs or slips affording convenient places for the loading and discharge of cargoes. Two avenues, China Street, and Hog Lane, intersect the space occupied by the Factories and stores; the first is a broad and handsome opening, having many well-furnished shops, the fronts of which are inscribed with mottos, calculated to attract customers, but not adorned in that fanciful and costly manner which prevails within the city-streets, from which, however, all foreigners are jealously excluded. Hog Lane possesses a totally different character — narrow, inconvenient, gloomy, occupied by the lowest classes, frequented only by persons of equally equivocal reputation, and frequently the scene of tumult, theft, and even assassination. Europeans are confined strictly to their own quarter or suburb, which hardly exceeds a few square yards in area, and the greater portion generally enjoy the refreshing breeze on the house-tops, whenever an aquatic excursion, which has always been tolerated, is inconvenient. There is a promenade called "Respondentia Walk," enclosed by railing, and forming an agreeable lounge, where merchants, commanders, and civil officers connected with the Factories, meet in the cool moments of evening; but, with the exception of this little terrace, there is not more space allowed to foreigners than is sufficient for the bonding or the standing of their goods, during the regular process of purchase, exchange, and shipping.

The two streets just mentioned divide the Hongs into three separate groups; the western, containing the French and Spanish Factories, along with the house of a Hanist or Chinese merchant who deals with foreigners; — the middle, the British, Danish, American, and Austrian; — the eastern, the Hong of the East India Company, the most graceful and architectural of all, being adorned with a portico and columns, and having a pleasure-ground railed round, and overlooking the river. Prohibition against entering the gates of the city, and strict confinement to the very limited and unhealthy space allotted to the foreigner, renders a lengthened residence here disagreeable to most persons, and intolerably humiliating to all, save the votaries of wealth and commerce.

---

[1] *The European factories comprised commercial agencies from over a dozen Western countries, amongst which the English East India Company (whose factory was founded at Canton in 1699) predominated. They were known to the Chinese as 'the barbarian houses'. The buildings were all destroyed in the course of the Opium War.*

[2] *'The Thirteen Hongs' was the name given to the Co-hong when it was reconstituted in 1782 and given the monopoly over all foreign trade at Canton and also made responsible for the behaviour of the foreigners. The inference above that the term refers to the European traders is incorrect.*

11
A Street in Canton

OLD Canton presents a specimen of street-life and street-habits in China, which may be received as a general representation of city scenes. From its very ancient foundation, and the long establishment of a productive commerce here, the population have outgrown the walled limits of the city, and a suburb of great extent has been added. The accompanying illustration, however, does not represent either the suburban or the European quarter, but strictly and truly a street of active business in the very heart of the ancient Chinese city of Quang-choo-foo. The extent of the original walls is only six miles, but the population of city and suburbs, together with the amphibious beings that dwell on board the junks on the Pearl river, is estimated at one million of souls.

Although the area within the walls is limited in extent, from the very contracted breadth of the avenues, as well as from the economy exercised in allotting ground for building, both streets and houses are surprisingly numerous, and the streets of Canton resemble flagged courts and passages, that afford so much convenience to the foot-passenger, every avenue being floored with spacious granite flags. In most instances, each street is contracted at its extremities to the breadth of a mere doorway; here a strong wooden valve, or iron gate, is hung, and here also is a guard-house, in which the night-watch is stationed. To these the care of the separate, single streets, is entrusted, to protect them against thieves, to give the alarm and assist in the event of fire, and to preserve the peace amongst the occupants themselves.

Deficiency of scientific knowledge in architecture, especially in the formation and support of the roof, has impeded the efforts of builders in China, so that the houses seldom rise higher than two stories; the houses of the richer classes are frequently of brick — of the less properous, of brick and wood, or of the latter only — but, of the poorest class, of unbaked clay or mud. Doors and windows stand open, protected from the weather by projecting eaves, and falling blinds, and fixed verandas. The wares are all exposed for sale with such confidence in public honesty, that the passenger experiences more familiarity and freedom from restraint in the trading streets of Canton, than inside the shops of London or Paris. Large umbrellas, the handle and the hood of bamboo, are spread wherever space permits, and a profitable trade is not unfrequently conducted beneath their grateful shelter. Lanterns are suspended over every door and window at nightfall; and, indeed, during the light of day, this Chinese emblem is seldom withdrawn. Either over the shop-window, or beside the door, *a sign* is usually placed, emblematic of the proprietor's calling, or in some way connected with the commercial history of the house.

The appearance of a Chinese street is agreeable, cheerful, picturesque: the people are intent on that object which constitutes the chief pursuit of mankind in general — riches; and their devotion to the cause is so entire, that dedicatory tablets to the god of wealth are hung up in many of their shops.

12
House of a
Chinese Merchant,
near Canton

That this plate is based on a drawing (by William Alexander) in the possession of Sir George Staunton is acknowledged below its title.

A CHINESE villa is an assemblage of buildings of various dimensions and designs, brought together without any apparent method, but displaying a fruitful imagination and an exhaustless fancy. The exterior parts are of that gloomy mural character, which prevails in all those countries where the softer sex are held in a mild but degrading imprisonment, by both parents and husbands; but within, the aspect at least, breathes pleasure and tranquillity. Although no regular order of art is discoverable in Chinese architecture, an analysis of its parts and comparison of examples will lead immediately to the detection of much system, and explain the necessity for what may appear superfluous. Having no idea of balancing materials according to those mathematical principles on which our great stone arches and sublime cathedrals are constructed, and continuing to lay the roofing-beams in a position at right angles to that adopted by our builders, they do not venture to form a roof of great span or dimensions. Since then he cannot have a broad roof, the Chinaman is content with a house in proportion; and if he possesses wealth enough to maintain a large establishment, instead of one great mansion, he causes many small buildings to be erected within the space enclosed for the seclusion and enjoyment of his family. The neccessary narrowness also of their roofs leaves no alternative, when a spacious apartment is required, but the introduction of pillars, hence the endless repetition of this feature in their houses. A veranda is sustained by pillars, behind which rises the main building, generally one story in height; but, when the grounds are so spacious that a second or third story may be raised, without affording the females of the family an opportunity of seeing or being seen, the addition is ofttimes made. In the southern provinces, where the original of the accompanying view exists, the veranda is essential for shade; the front of each apartment is open, save the intervention of a lattice-work gilt and brightly painted; and even in the upper rooms, the door is the only medium of light and air. The pillars which sustain the roof of every apartment are of pine wood, sometimes carved, more frequently plain but painted, and the rafters are covered with glazed tiles, of a concave form, and laid like roofing tiles in England; the bright blue colour of the bricks in the walls is relieved by scrolling and seaming of white paint, with an excellent effect. Whether Europeans view the Chinese roof as a beauty or deformity, it is upon this part of the building the architect expends his best abililties. The gables are grotesquely adorned with scroll-work and gilded dragons; nor is his license limited, unless by the variety of patterns which the flowers of the field, the birds of the air, and the beasts of the forest include. But the genius of the artist must extend beyond mere architectural decoration; he must also be able to introduce within the villa an artificial lake, adorn its banks with rock-work and pleasure-grounds, and associate the wildest productions of untamed nature with the most gorgeous creations of art. Bridges, canals, fountains, grottos, rocks worn or wrought into the most extravagant forms, and either insulated in the water or starting from the flower-beds, are the usual objects with which villa pleasure-grounds are decorated; and the fancy that is displayed in their disposition, to foreigners must necessarily appear most admirable, and is amazingly difficult of successful imitation.

13
City of Amoy from the Tombs

CAPTAIN Stoddart's[1] accurate view of the site and scenery of this celebrated entrepôt, is a panorama of exquisite loveliness. Employing the ancient burial-ground as an observatory, the eye ranges over the low-lying city with its battlements, the widespread suburbs, with their countless cottages; beyond these, again, to the land-locked cove, dotted with busy merchant-men, there riding securely from every breath of wind. Above the waters of the inner bay, which closely resembles an inland lake, rises a noble chain of mountains, dentated in outline, and granitic in structure. Ko-long-soo,[2] interposed between the outward ocean and this picturesque basin, acts as a natural and most efficient breakwater, imparting such entire and constant placidity to its surface, that vessels may lie here at all seasons regardless of the weather, biding their time for unfurling the sails; and transit from shore to shore by boats of tiny tonnage, is never attended with risk or interruption. It seems, therefore, reasonable to conclude that the island and city of Amoy will succeed to a large share of that trade, which is hourly passing away from Canton for ever.[3] The navigation of the Canton river is tedious, and often insecure, — the entrance to the cove of Amoy is short, deep, and unimpeded. Departure is equally inconvenient from the former city, while vessels may wait in the inner harbour of Amoy, under island-shelter, for favourable weather, and sail almost the moment of its return. Besides these natural advantages, our embassies and expeditions have uniformly found a more generous feeling, predominant at Amoy, towards foreigners, and traders, and visitors, than at other ports of China; and it is sufficiently shown by our missionaries and travellers, that the citizens of this populous place would long since have saluted the British flag, floating on the tranquil bosom of their sun-lit bay, if Peking's threats had not deterred them from every act of hospitality to the stranger.

Being nearer to Canton than the other open-ports of the empire, Amoy will probably be sooner, as well as more securely, enriched, by the abolition of commercial monopoly at that much-disliked emporium; and, from the very flattering accounts given by Gutzlaff,[4] Medhurst,[5] and other learned travellers, of the social character of its citizens, intercourse with foreigners at this city is likely to be more close, more constant, and more conciliatory, than has ever hitherto been permitted by this very jealous people.

---

[1] *For Stoddart, refer to the Introduction.*

[2] *Kolongsu is the smaller of the two islands on which the city of Amoy stands. During the Treaty Port period, it was the residential quarter of the Western traders living at Amoy.*

[3] *This perhaps reflects wishful thinking on the part of the writer who obviously shared the jaundiced view of Canton held by most Englishmen of that city, as a result of its virulent hostility towards Britons both during and after the first Opium War.*

[4] *Karl Gutzlaff, 'the Prussian buccaneer missionary interpreter' (as described by Arthur Waley) was on account of his knowledge of Chinese appointed magistrate of Tinghai, and then of Ningpo, during the British administration.*

[5] *Medhurst (later Sir Walter) was the high-handed British Consul-General in Shanghai in the 1860s who later became regarded as an expert on things Chinese.*

14
West Gate of Ching-keang-foo[1]

WHERE the Imperial Canal enters the Yang-tse-kiang river on the south, and where a broad and beautiful natural harbour is formed by the river's winding course, a vast trade has been contracted, and large cities have grown up. In the centre of the river, at its widest part, stands the Golden Island,[2] clothed to its tapering summit with the most luxuriant foliage; on the northern shore is seated the city of Quangtchou,[3] and, on the southern Ching-keang-foo. Ridge after ridge of rocky mountains stretches away from the borders of the bay into the remotest distance, producing a remarkable contrast of imagined retirement and sterility, with the smiling and animated picture which the river, here a league[4] in breadth, presents to the eye. The surface is varied by the presence of vessels, differing in size, shape, and objects. Some sailing with, others against the current; many crossing from one opening of the canal to the opposite; and countless numbers lying at anchor.

Ching-keang-foo being the key to the southern provinces, the out-port on which Nanking depends for its security against foreign aggression, was deemed of corresponding importance to the British troops in the subjugation of the Chinese empire. Being strongly protected by walls, thirty feet in height, and five in thickness, containing a large and active population, and being garrisoned by a body of resolute Tartars, its reduction was considered both the more necessary and more glorious to our army. Ascending the canal, and effecting a safe landing on both sides of the water, at the foot of a lofty and noble bridge of one arch, the British commenced a vigorous assault upon the west gate of the city. A much warmer reception than was anticipated, at first threw the assailants into some confusion, and the Blonde's[5] boats, after a desperate resistance, were actually for a while in the enemy's hands. From this perilous position, however, they were soon released, by a party of marines and seamen belonging to the Cornwallis.[5]

This momentary setback only lent new resolution to those who were its victims; and, under cover of a destructive fire from the opposite bank of the canal, Captain Richardson led up a scaling party to the walls. Rockets and heavy guns soon overthrew the gate-towers, and the gates themselves becoming a mass of flame, destroyed all prospect of future resistance. Submission now was the sole remaining portion of the Tartars, who had fought with courage and devotion.

Only four miles in circuit, Ching-keang-foo is but a minor city, indeed it is the fifth in magnitude in Kiang-nan; however, from its geographical position, it is always esteemed one of the first in commercial rank. The streets are narrow, paved with marble, and contain many well-supplied shops, in which horn for lanterns forms a prominent article of sale; and the suburbs are nearly equal to the enclosed city in extent.

---

[1] *Chinkiang is a city two thousand years old. It was the scene of the sharpest fighting and the largest British casualties of the Opium War. Its loss, which threatened Peking's food supplies, persuaded the Manchu Government to make peace. The spot where the British fleet anchored is now covered by villages and rice-fields, the river having changed its course.*

[2] *Golden Island, a picturesque and mountainous island midstream, was made famous by the visits of the K'ang-hsi and Ch'ien-lung (Qianlong) Emperors during their respective reigns.*

[3] *Quang-tchou probably refers to Yangchow, fifteen miles north of Chinkiang on the Grand Canal, a city famous for its wealth and its women. Marco Polo was its Governor for three years.*

[4] *About three miles.*

[5] *The* Blonde *and* Cornwallis *were warships, part of the British fleet, under Admiral Parker.*

15
City of Ning-po, from the River

ABOUT twelve miles from the archipelago of Chusan, and on the left bank of the Ta-hea, or Kin river, stands the walled city of Ning-po,[1] which Europeans formerly called Liam-po. It is the fourth city of the province of Tche-kiang, is itself of the first order, having four of the third under its jurisdiction, and enjoys the advantage of a good roadstead. Seated at the confluence of two rivers, the Ta-hea and Yao, its position is both agreeable and convenient; and the trade between this port and Japan has always been of an active character. A very level plain surrounds the site of Ning-po, extending to a distance of many miles on every side, and confined ultimately to the form of a vast oval basin, by lofty mountains, that rise abruptly and terminate the view. Many towns speckle the smooth surface of these fertile fields, on which also vast numbers of cattle are fed, and luxuriant crops of rice, cotton, and pulse are raised. Nowhere in China is irrigation more advantageously or more skilfully adopted, than in the rich plain of Ning-po, the waters that descend from the encircling mountains being directed into sixty-six canals, all which, after contributing their services to the duty of fertilizing, discharge their surplus into a main trunk that communicates with the Ta-hea. The amphitheatre of hills, the luxuriant vegetation of the well-watered plain, the occurrence of so many comfortable-looking towns, the brilliant sky, the wholesome and salubrious climate, and the great variety of trees, combine in the formation of a picture whose character is the most happy and agreeable. "The scenery about Ning-po," writes commander Bingham, "formed the prettiest landscape we had seen in China."

Its walls, extending rather more than five miles, are entirely of granite; and five gates afford admission within them. There are also two watergates, these are mere arches in the walls, through which canals pass, each being protected by a portcullis. The public buildings are mean, and few in number, trade having for ages so completely absorbed the attention of the citizens, that the fine arts fell into oblivion. One lofty pagoda of brick, is the sole architectural boast of the place;[2] and a bridge of boats over the Ta-hea, constructed about three centuries back, still retains its position. The streets are rather broader than those of Canton, and the shops better furnished, especially with japan-ware; but their width suffers an apparent diminution from the pent-houses which project beyond the shop-fronts. In the early years of the last century the English were permitted to trade here; but the intrigues of the Portuguese and Russians, combined with the bigotry of the Chinese, deprived them of that valuable privilege, and restricted their merchants to the ports of Canton and Macao. To this advantage, however, our commerce is restored by the treaty signed after the conclusion of the opium war; and Ning-po for many years has participated more largely in foreign trade, exchanging her silks, cottons, teas, and lacquered-ware, for the woollens and hardware of England, than any other of the free ports of the empire.[3]

---

[1]*Ningpo, another ancient city, was the site of one of the earliest Portuguese settlements on the China coast (1522), until they were expelled in the 1540s. The English East India Company opened a factory at neighbouring Tinghai in 1698, hoping to develop trade with Ningpo, but was disappointed and so withdrew.*

[2]*These disparaging remarks on Ningpo's architectural attractions are rather unfair; the city possessed several remarkable temples and guild houses and the pagoda alluded to is presumably the Heaven-Invested Pagoda, built in AD 696 and one of the oldest in China. It will be noticed that in the picture there is more than one pagoda.*

[3]*Ningpo was one of the five 'Treaty Ports' named in the Treaty of Nanking as being opened to British trade (the others — Canton, Amoy, Foochow (Fuzhou) and Shanghai). However, Ningpo was soon overshadowed by Shanghai as a centre of trade.*

16
Ancient Bridge, Chapoo[1]

THE flat bridge of a single opening on the river of Chapoo is obviously of the most early style. Strong abutments being constructed, large flags are laid, lapping one over the other like stairs, to the edge, or nearly, of the pier, from which flag-stones of requisite dimensions are laid across the interval. In the next era of bridge-building the Egyptian arch was adopted; in the third, the segment of a perfect circle.

On the balustrade of Chapoo bridge, lions couchant, rather rudely executed, are placed, emblematic of the magnificence of the structure, or the great ability of the architect. In no country is learning held in higher esteem, art pursued with greater zeal, or genius more uniformly rewarded. The captain of a Tartar band, who succeeds in annihilating or dispersing a gang of bandits, is honoured with a triumphal arch, on which his exploits are blazoned in letters of gold; temples are raised to the memory of the philosopher; and the fame of the artist is perpetuated by various types of national monument. The engineer of the great tunnel at Nanking is ever before the eyes and the minds of his countrymen, a memorial to his honour being placed on the highest pinnacle of the mountain which the tunnel pierces. The memory of their princes is also preserved by architectural testimonials, inferior, however, in most instances, to the monuments of those whom science or virtue has rendered illustrious. Although women are secluded from public life in China, they are treated with the utmost tenderness, their lords pretending, that it is solely with a view to spare their feelings, that they do not require them to participate in the active duties of society. Whether this be a specimen of Chinese duplicity, or a true and genuine sentiment, it is certain that the highest honours are frequently paid to female virtue, and the praises of the softer sex are not only celebrated in the stanzas of the poet, but obelisks and arches, and monuments of the most costly character, are also raised, to mark a nation's admiration of the high qualities that distinguish mother, wife, and daughter.

---

[1] *The small town Chapu, of ancient vintage, occupied a strategic point on Hangchow Bay, and was therefore the object of a British naval attack. The fighting at Chapu was almost as severe as that which took place at Chinkiang two months later; the British lost 9 men with 50 wounded against some 1,500 Chinese casualties.*

17
The City of Nanking

NANKING,[1] the capital of Kiang-nan, was formerly the metropolis of the empire, and one of the finest cities in the world, and its population, when it was the Imperial residence, has been estimated at three millions. Several canals form an easy communication with the Yang-tse-kiang; and large barges, and Imperial luggage-junks, navigate them with the most perfect facility. The famous pirate, or rather patriot, Cosinga,[2] having sailed up the river, entered the canal, and laid siege to Nanking, it was deemed advisable, on his retirement, to block up the entrance of the latter, so as to obstruct the passage of all vessels of war. The example of the gallant conqueror of Formosa, however, was not lost upon the British; who, in the Chinese war of 1840, pursued precisely a similar policy, penetrating also to the ramparts of Nanking.

The spacious *enceinte* of the walls is of an irregular outline, and varied by plain and mountain, the latter, like the castle-hill of Edinburgh, impending over the public ways. One third, at least, of the whole area, now lies desolate; the palaces, temples, observatories, and imperial sepulchres, having all been ruined or demolished by the Tartars. A city of the first class, Nanking is the residence of a great mandarin, (Tsong-tou,)[3] a viceroy presiding over the two Keang provinces,[4] to whom an appeal lies, in all important matters, from the tribunals of the East and West divisions. The fierce Tartars, whose ancestors spoiled Nanking of its splendour, and transferred the seat of empire to the Northern capital, still guard with jealousy the actions of the native inhabitants in this, their ancient capital; and, a strong Tartar garrison, under the command of a general of their own nation, constantly occupies a sort of barrack or citadel, separated from the rest of the city by strong battlements. The streets, in general, are narrow and inconvenient; the public buildings contemptible, with the exception of the city gates, which here, as well as in many of the principal cities, are remarkably fantastic and beautiful, and of the public monuments, erected by imperial command, to perpetuate the fame of a favourite.

Retaining their industry, which seems to have received a new impulse by the withdrawal of the vain, and idle, and dependent attachés of an imperial court the Nanking manufacturers have brought their labours to the highest degree of excellence. The satins, plain and flowered, made here, are most esteemed at Peking, even those of Canton being postponed and sold at lower prices; the cotton cloth woven here, and bearing the name of the city, has long been admired in Europe; rice paper, and artificial flowers, formed from the pith of a leguminous plant called *Tong-tsao*, constitute also a very important part of the prevailing manufactures. At *Hoei-tcheou*, in the province of Kiang-nan, the celebrated "Indian ink," so much prized in England, is manufactured; but it is sold for exportation principally at Nanking.

In this ancient city, learning also has long been seated, and a larger proportion of doctors, and great mandarins, and distinguished scholars, is sent hence to Peking and its colleges, than from any other city in the empire. Public libraries are numerous — the trade of a bookseller particularly respected — printing better understood than elsewhere in China, and the paper of Nanking is almost a miracle amongst national manufactures.

---

[1] *Nanking has served in several periods as the capital of China, the most recent being under the Kuomintang regime of Generalissimo Chiang Kai-shek before the Japanese invasion of 1937.*

[2] *Koxinga or Cheng Ch'eng-kung — a Chinese rebel leader who aimed to restore the Ming dynasty; the attempt was blunted by his failure to take Nanking in 1657. After this he continued his campaign from Formosa (Taiwan), from which he expelled the Dutch, until his death in 1662.*

[3] *Tsong-tou* (tsung-tu), *Governor-General (not viceroy).*

[4] *Kiangsu and Anhwei: see note on p.9.*

18
The Bridge of Nanking

NANKING is not seated immediately on the banks of the Yangste-keang, but at the distance of three miles from them, and connected with that noble river by a wide and deep canal; so considerable indeed is this artificial navigation, which continues parallel to the west and south walls of the city, at a trifling interval only, that the bridges thrown across it are works of much architectual pretentions. Near to the foot of the Porcelain Tower,[1] the largest and principal bridge of Nanking spans the main trunk of the canal, forming a communication between an extensive suburb, and the west gate of the city. It consists of six well-turned arches of unequal width, and is kept down nearly to a level with the banks at either extremity.

Chinese bridges are constructed on different principles, in different parts of the empire. Arches, pointed like the Early English, may be found in one locality; the horse-shoe, or Moorish form, abounds in another: ornamental bridges, in gardens and pleasure-grounds, consist mostly of one opening, either arched or flat; some of those built over navigable rivers have piers so lofty, that junks of two hundred tons burden can sail under them without striking their masts; one arch, and of large dimensions, is of frequent occurrence; so also are bridges of a number of arches, and that near Sou-tchoo-foo consists of no fewer than ninety-one.

That beauty and strength are not inseparable in works of art, is at least fully illustrated in the structure of the graceful one-arch bridge of China. Each stone is cut so as to form the segment of a circle, and, as there is no keystone, ribs of wood, fitted to the convexity of the arch, are bolted through the stones by iron bars, fastened securely into the dead-work of the bridge. Sometimes wood is dispensed with, in which case the curved stones are mortised into long transverse blocks of the same material. In some parts of the empire, on the other hand, arches of smaller stones, and pointed to a centre, as in Europe, are everywhere seen. The arches of the towers on the Great Wall, are all exactly turned, and the masonry of that miracle of labour is referred to by those who have examined it, as a perfect model of permanent engineering.

The Bridge of Nanking is built entirely of red granite, with circular arches turned with cuneiformed stones, and resting on piers of solid masonry. That its projectors were little apprehensive for its stability, is shown by the erection on each side of the causeway, of a row of substantial dwellings, one story in height. These do not prove as injurious as droves of cattle, coaches driven at a rapid pace, or armies marching with regulated step, the most severe test of a swinging bridge, but they do, to a certain extent, establish the sustaining ability of the structure. On one side of Nanking great bridge is shown the city wall, on the other the Porcelain Tower; while the state-junk, conveying an imperial commissioner, who had just arrived to treat with the English, has reached its berth at the principal landing-place.[2]

---

[1] *The famed and beautiful Porcelain Pagoda built by the third Ming ruler, the Emperor Yung-lo (1402–24), in honour of his mother. It was destroyed during the Great Taiping Rebellion which followed the Opium War. The Taiping rebels captured Nanking in 1853, and occupied it as their capital for the next eleven years.*

[2] *The occasion of this picture was the signing of the Treaty of Nanking in 1842 which ended the First Opium War. The Imperial Commissioner in question was the Manchu Ch'i-ying (Kiying).*

19
The Western Gate of Peking[1]

This picture is based (although not acknowledged) on that done by William Alexander in 1799, after his return with the Macartney embassy from China. The main difference is in the perspective.

PEKING, the capital of the Chinese empire, is situated in a fertile plain, about fifty miles from the Great Wall, in the province of Pe-tcheli, and on the Yu-ho, a tributary to the Pei-ho about fifteen miles eastward of the city. Its form is that of a rectangle or right-angled parallelogram, having an area of about fourteen square miles, exclusive of extensive suburbs, divided into two totally distinct and separate sections; the northern, a perfect square, founded by the Mantchoos, is inhabited by Tartars exclusively, and includes the imperial palace: the southern, in the form of a parallelogram, is occupied solely by Chinese. Each city is enclosed by its respective walls, the enceinte of one series covering nine square miles; of the other, the imperial, or Tartar, occupying five. These defences, like those of other cities of the first class, consist of walls about thirty feet in height and twenty in thickness. Two retaining walls, the bases of stone, the upper parts of brick, having a considerable slope on the exterior, but perpendicular within, were first raised, and the interval afterwards filled up with earth. The summit between the parapets is levelled, floored with tiles, and access to it afforded by inclined planes enclosed within the thickness of the walls.

The south wall[2] is pierced by three gates of entrance, the others, by two each; whence the origin of the name, "the City of Nine Gates." The walls, on which twelve horsemen may ride abreast, are finished with parapets, indented with irregular gun-pits, for in fact the Manchu soldier depends on his bow. For more complete security and defence,

in front of each entrance is an esplanade enclosed by a semicircular curtain, and used as a "place of arms." The entrance to the esplanade is not immediately in front of the inner gate, but lateral, a plan adopted in European fortresses; and the battlements above are unprotected by any implements of war. Above and behind these great bastions rise pavilion-roofed watch-towers, of nine stories each, and pierced with port-holes; these, however, are not available in cases of sudden emergency, for the forms which they present are unreal, the cannon shown in each aperture being only painted, sham. The walls are pierced by numerous loop-holes for the discharge of arrows, and a similar policy is adopted on the mural ramparts, where the embrasures are unoccupied by cannon, but openings for archery are formed in the wall. At equal intervals, some sixty yards, the distance at which a Tartar's bow proves fatal, stand flanking-towers, projecting from the curtain-wall about forty feet. These are similar in design, and equal in height, to the great structures that command the gates. Two principal streets, a hundred feet in width, and four miles in length, connect the northern and southern gates, and two of corresponding breadth extend from east to west.

[1] *The Ping-tze Men, the more central of the two gates on the west wall of the Tartar City, which was used frequently by Lord Macartney and his entourage on their way to and from the audience hall at Yuen-min-Yuen or Old Summer Palace. The avenue from the gate led directly to the Imperial City within the Tartar City. This and other gates in the city walls were destroyed in the 1950s.*

[2] *Of the Tartar City.*

20
Hong-kong, from Kow-loon

This engraving, based on a sketch by Captain Stoddart in 1841, shows the scene at least a decade later, by which time Hong Kong had acquired the substantial buildings seen on the waterfront. The point at which Stoddart drew his sketch was Tsim Sha Tsui, Kowloon.

HONG-KONG, or Heong-keong, land of crystal streams, at a distance appears, like all others of "the thousand islands" that stud the estuary of the Tigris[1] — precipitous and uninviting. Its high hills often terminate in sharp peaks, and are thickly strewn with masses of rock, of primitive formation, frequently piled upon one another in a remarkable and sometimes fantastic manner, with here and there a lower hill, covered with gravel and sand. From the summit to the water's edge there are few or no trees; and, except in the months of May, June, July, and August, when these islands look green, they might be supposed to be quite barren.

Victoria is the only town on the island; this was founded by the English, in 1841, and formally ceded to the British crown under the Nanking treaty. In the short term of two years from Sir H. Pottinger's[2] arrival, when a tent was pitched for the government-residence, a large town has sprung up, a dense population has accumulated. Here now are to be seen extensive stores, forts, wide streets, bazaars, and markets. A noble military road, sixteen yards broad, has been constructed, and continued entirely round the island. Branch roads to Tie-tam* and Chuck-py-wan,* traverse the hills, exhibiting in their formation the most scientific modes of civil engineering practised in Europe. The list of public buildings includes a government-house, jail, court-house, church, Baptist chapel, a Catholic establishment, Morrison's Education Society,[3] medical missionaries', and mariners' hospitals. Including the Chinese quarter, situated east of the governor's house, the total population amounts to 14,000 souls.

The village of Chek-choo,* the largest and most important on the island, contains 800 inhabitants. There are 180 dwellings and shops at this place, and the average value of each house is 400 dollars. The houses at Chek-choo, although inferior to those in an ordinary Chinese town on the mainland, are yet superior to those found in the other villages of Hong-kong; but the quality of land under cultivation, as well as the quantity, is not equal to that at Heong-kong,* Wang-nie-chong,* Soo-kun-poo,* and Pok-foo-lum,* places that may be strictly denominated agricultural villages.

The other villages on the island, besides Chek-choo, are — Heong-kong, from which the island derives its name, prettily enclosed in trees, surrounded by cultivated land, and having about 200 inhabitants. Tie-tam is situated at the head of a deep bay, where a good deal of flat land may be reclaimed, and a good boat-harbour formed. A few ships may find protection from the weather in particular parts of the bay of Tie-tam; but the other parts are exposed in both monsoons. Some fifty poor people dwell here. Wang-nie-chong and Soo-kun-poo are picturesquely placed in the midst of fruit-trees, and surrounded by cultivated land. In their vicinity, as at Tie-tam, a considerable extent of land might be reclaimed from the sea, and it shortly will be much required for building-purposes. The united population of the two villages amounts to about 350. Pok-foo-lum is situated about 500 feet above the level of the sea, and commands an extensive view of all the islands to the south and west, as far as Macao. There are, besides the villages enumerated, many hamlets on the east coast of the island, where the magnificent granite of Hong-kong is principally quarried.

---

[1] *Tigris was the Portuguese name for the Pearl River.*

[2] *Sir Henry Pottinger took over from Captain Charles Elliott as Chief Superintendent of Trade during the Opium War and became the first Governor of Hong Kong.*

[3] *This society for educating Chinese children in Hong Kong was the legacy of J.R. Morrison who served as interpreter during the War and was the son of the Revd. Robert Morrison, the first British Protestant missionary to China.*

*The identification of these Hong Kong villages in Cantonese is as follows: Chek-choo (Chek-chü), now Stanley; Chuck-py-wan (Shek Pai Wan), near Aberdeen; Heong-Kong, no longer identifiable, Pok-foo-lum (Pok Fu Lam); Soo-kun-poo (So Kon Po); Tie-tam (Tai Tam); Wang-nie-chong (Wong Nei Chong). See map on p. 41.

21 Harbour of Hong-Kong[1]

VICTORIA

SO KON PO

POK FU LAM

WONG NEI CHONG

HONG KONG

SHEK PAI WAN (ABERDEEN)

TAI TAM

CHEK-CHU (STANLEY)

THE ISLAND OF HONG KONG

As a commercial entrepôt, as a safe asylum for our shipping in the Oriental seas, as commanding the estuary of the Canton river, and as a military station, Hong-Kong possesses the utmost value; but, it never can become a port for the direct and immediate shipment of Chinese exports, the mountainous and inhospitable character of the coast between it and the productive provinces of the empire, rendering communication difficult. The harbour, however, the subject of the accompanying view, is one of the noblest roadsteads in the east; situated between the north-west extremity of the island and the mainland, it may be entered southward through Lamma Channel, — westward by the Cap-sing-mun passage, and from the east by vessels sailing close under the peninsula of Kow-lung. When Captain Elliott's[2] proclamation declared Hong-Kong to be a part and parcel of the British dominions, he marked out the site of Queen's-Town[3] on the southern shore, and here, around the standard of freedom, whole streets started into existence as if raised by the wand of the enchanter. A broad hard road now extends to the harbour of Ty-tam, around which marine villas are in progress of erection, commanding the grand spectacle of Hong harbour, and enjoying the refreshing breezes that blow from the unbounded sea. At the base of the lofty mountain-chain that margins the Chinese coast for many a league, is the Cow-loon (kow-lung, *the winding dragon*) peninsula, which, like the isthmus at Gibraltar, was to have been considered neutral ground, but the Chinese having violated the treaty, it was seized by the British, who garrisoned the fort and named it Victoria, in honour of her Britannic majesty.[4]

---

[1] *This view is probably taken from the mainland opposite Stonecutter's Island. Mystery surrounds the origin of the name of Hong Kong, but the Revd. Wright's suggestion that it came from the name of a torrent on the island known as* heang-keang *(fragrant stream) or* hoong-keang *(red or bright torrent) was one of the earliest, and as good an explanation as any.*

[2] *Captain Charles Elliott (cousin of Rear-Admiral George Elliott) was the Superintendent of Trade at Canton when the First Opium War broke out. His proclamation of the annexation of Hong Kong came about as the result of the signing of the Convention of Chuenpi in January 1841.*

[3] *The first name given to Victoria.*

[4] *Fort Victoria, see p. 57.*

III
CHINESE
LANDSCAPES

Like everything else in China, the landscapes were different — to Western eyes. The scenes which follow are hardly representative of the whole country since they only touch those fringes to which Westerners had access. Nevertheless they contributed towards creating the stereotyped Western images of the Chinese world — a world peopled by folk who were to be found everywhere doing everything against a background of placid waterways and fantastic mountain peaks, rivers crowded with all means of craft but overshadowed by the broad-hulked and square sailed junks, towns with pillared houses and ornate roofs pierced here and there by tall pagodas, all protected by the spectacular and unique Great Wall.

22
Bamboo Aqueduct
at Hong-kong

THE surface of Hong-kong is undulating, the climate sultry, the soil shallow; of the first feature, advantage has been taken by encouraging the growth of timber in the glens, within which the loveliest hamlets may be seen enclosed; the shade and the shelter of foliage offsets, in some degree, the ferocity of a tropical sun; and, industry, unequalled in any other kingdom, has converted a soil the most discouraging into one the most productive. It is for agricultural purposes, chiefly, that such primitive contrivances as the bamboo aqueduct are employed; but the value and utility of this tree are so universally understood in the eastern parts of Asia, that, even were other materials present, they very probably would be rejected.

The bamboo-cane is a very beautiful and a very elegant species of plant, hollow, round, straight, having knots on the stem at every ten or twelve inches, alternate branches, spear-shaped leaves, and sometimes attaining a height of forty feet. A native of the tropical regions of both hemispheres, it however attains more complete maturity in the east, where it is held in the highest estimation, and devoted to infinite uses. We have shown in the illustration that the stem, when bored, is made a conduit for water. Besides serving for aqueducts from hill to hill, bridges to continue land-transit are successfully and gracefully formed of this beautiful tree.

23
The Great Wall
of China[1]

BEFORE the Mantchoo Tartars subjugated China Proper, the Great Wall, one of the most gigantic conceptions that ever occupied the human intellect, was the northern boundary of the empire; and it owes its foundation to Chi-Hoang-Ti, of the fourth Tsin dynasty, who was the first ruler of a united China.[2] Finding the petty princes of Tartary troublesome to his frontier subjects, he sent an army against the former, and drove them into the recesses of their mountains, and employed the latter, during this interval of rest, in building a rampart to exclude all freebooters for the future.

The eastern end of Chi-Hoang's wall extends into the Gulf of Lea ou-tong, in the same latitude nearly as Peking. It consists of huge blocks of granite, resting on piles or pedestals supposed to be composed of the hulks of ships filled with iron, which the emperor caused to be sunk in the sea as a secure foundation. Extending westward, its fronts are finished with such exactitude that a nail could not be driven between them. The style of building resembles that exhibited in the walls of Peking, and of other fortified cities, the dimensions, however, being considerably greater. Its average height is twenty feet, including five feet of parapet rising from the platform or rampart, which is fifteen from the ground-level. The thickness at the base is twenty-five feet, and on the platform fifteen. The structure consists of two front or retaining walls, two feet in thickness, the interval being filled up with earth, rubble-stone, or other loose material. To the height of six feet, the fronts are of hewn granite; the upper part entirely of sun-dried brick of a blue colour. The platform, which is paved with brick, is approached by stairs of the same material, or of stone, ascending so gradually that horses do not refuse to tread them. In the province of Pecheli,

the wall is terraced, and cased with brick; as it enters Chensi it begins to be of inferior workmanship, sometimes only of earth; but, on the side of Cha-hou-keou, to which the Muscovite merchants[3] come direct from Siberia, it is again of stone and brick, with large strong towers always garrisoned. From this point southward, military posts are erected along the banks of the Hoang-ho, in which guards are maintained, to keep the boundary between the neighbouring provinces of Chan-si and Chen-si, and prevent the navigation of the river by hostile tribes. Passing the Hoang-ho into the province of Chen-si, the wall is generally of earth, in some places quite obliterated, but, in remarkable passes it is defended by either towers or large towns, where military mandarins, with a strong force, are usually stationed.

Notwithstanding the frail character of the materials in several places, this great national work, fifteen hundred miles in extent, has undoubtedly endured for two thousand years, with but indifferent care and little restoration: Wherever a river was to be passed, an arch or arches of solid masonry was thrown across, protected by iron-grating, that dipped a little into the waters, and effectually obstructed entry, where mountains occurred, the wall was made to climb their most rugged fronts, and in one instance reaches an elevation of five thousand feet above the sea. Wherever the nature of the ground rendered invasion easy, there the wall is double, treble, or as manifold as the necessity of the case would appear to demand.

The principal gates are fortified only on the side of China, and there protected by large flanking towers; at intervals of every hundred yards along the wall stand embattlements, forty feet square at the base, thirty at the height of the platform of the wall, and having sometimes one, sometimes two stories, above it.

---

[1] *This classical view is taken from a point near Peking.*

[2] *Ch'in Shih Huang-ti (Qin Shi Huangdi), the ruler of the frontier state of Ch'in (Qin), brought the other Chinese states under his control and proclaimed himself the first Emperor of China in 221 BC.*

[3] *Traders from Moscow; the Russians had established regular trading relations with Manchu China since the Treaty of Nerchinsk, signed in 1689.*

24
Junks Passing an Inclined Plane on the Imperial Canal

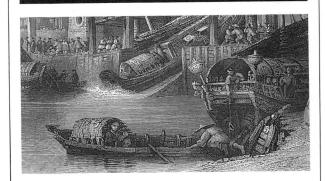

This picture is an adaptation by Allom of a drawing by William Alexander. The scene is wrongly ascribed to a view of the Imperial Canal on which ramps as shown here do not exist. Alexander's drawing was of a junction of waterways near Ningpo.

HOWEVER men of science, or well-read travellers, may look down upon the the Imperial Canal,[1] it is one of the most conspicuous monuments of manual labour in existence. It does not penetrate mountains by means of tunnels, or cross vast vales by aqueducts, but, preferring the level which nature presents, it traverses half the length of the empire, having a breadth and depth that have not been attempted in any other stillwater navigation in the world. In some places, its width, at the surface, is a thousand feet, in none is it less than two hundred; and, when a low level is to be crossed, this is effected by embankments, lined with stone walls of marble or granite, enclosing a volume of water that flows with a velocity of about three miles an hour, and always amply supplied. When the canal has to accomplish an ascent of any great length, the builders appear to have commenced their labours in the middle of the slope, and, by cutting down the higher part, and elevating the lower, reduced the whole to the required, or chosen level. These cuttings, however, never exceed fifty feet in depth, nor do the elevations in any instance surpass that height. Only despotic power could have compressed so great a quantity of human labour within any reasonable space of time, even in a country where the physical power of millions can be put in operation with considerable facility. But in China, it is found that the greatest works are still executed by the concentration of manual labour, unaided by machinery, except when mechanical power is absolutely necessary to be combined in its operation with human strength. The descent of the Imperial Canal from the highlands to the low-country, is not effected by locks, but by lengthened stages, or levels, falling like steps, from station to station, the height of the falls ranging from six to ten feet. At these floodgates the water is maintained at the upper level by planks let down one upon another, in grooves cut in the side-posts; and two solid abutments, or jetties, enclose the inclined plane, up or down which the junk is to pass. On the jetties are constructed powerful capstans, worked by levers, to which a number of hands can be conveniently applied, and, by these combinations of animal and mechanical power, the largest junks that navigate the canal, with their full cargoes, are raised or lowered. Dexterity is required in guiding the junk through the floodgate, and while passing the plane, an inclination of forty-five degrees: to accomplish these objects, a helmsman, with one weighty oar, is stationed at the prow, while bargemen, standing on the jetties, let down fenders of skin stuffed with hair, to save the junk from injury, should she touch the side-walls in her rapid transit. As the loss of water is considerable, and the means of checking the discharge both tedious and clumsy, the floodgates are opened at stated hours only; then all the vessels to be passed are ranged in order, and raised or lowered with astonishing rapidity, A toll paid by each laden barge is levied for the repairs of the moveable dams, and for the fees of the keepers.

---

[1] *The Imperial or Grand Canal, finally completed during the reign of the Mongol Emperor Kublai Khan (1260–91), runs from Hangchow to Tientsin, a distance of 650 miles.*

25
Entrance to the Hoang-ho, or Yellow River[1]

This is another adaptation of an Alexander drawing. The scene shown here is of the old estuary which debouched into the Yellow Sea. In 1852 the river changed its course and now flows into the Gulf of Chih-li (Bohai), four hundred miles further north.

ISSUING from two spacious lakes, Tcharing and Oring, at Sing-suh-hae, in the lofty mountains of Thibet, and in the region of Kokonor, the waters of Hoang-ho descend from their source, at first, through a length of two hundred and fifty miles, with the most uncontrollable impetuosity; then turning from an eastern to a north-western direction, they find a more level course for about an equal distance, after which they enter the Chinese province of Shan-tse, and the stream, remaining parallel in its course for some hundred miles with the Great Wall, at length intersects that celebrated work in the twenty-ninth degree of latitude, and takes a northern direction for upwards of four hundred additional miles. Hence, many rivers and lakes contributing the overflow of their waters to swell those of the great recipient, and again directing its power eastward, it recrosses the Great Wall, traverses the northern provinces for hundreds of miles further, and enters Honan in the same parallel of latitude in which it has its source. In Kiang-nan it is augmented by a vast contribution from Lake Hong-tse, after which the majestic volume moves more slowly towards that part of the eastern ocean to which it imparts both its turbid character and expressive name.

It is its intersection with the imperial canal — the junction of Lake Hong-tse, the afflux of the Salt river — that is considered to be the mouth of the Hoang-ho; and here it is that commerce has formed a rendezvous for shipping, and here also superstition has erected an altar to her worship. Descending with rapidity through a constant slope, of two thousand five hundred miles, the stream of the Hoang-ho acquires a momentum that renders the crossing from shore to shore always a perilous undertaking. At the mouth of Lake Hong-tse, and at the precise spot where the canal locks into the river, the velocity of the current is seldom less than four miles an hour, although that locality is not more than twenty miles distant from the sea. It has been calculated from the breadth, mean depth, and velocity that this famous river discharges into the Yellow sea in every hour of fleeting time, 2,563,000,000 gallons of water, which is more than one thousand times as much as the Ganges yields. The quantity of mud which it constantly holds in suspension, and which it carries with it into the sea is in such proportion as to disfigure its brightness, and give it amongst geographers a characteristic name.

---

[1] *The Yellow River, sometimes referred to as the 'Sorrow of China' on account of its destructive floods, is virtually unnavigable because of its shallowness and swiftly-changing currents. The three-mile broad estuary was so treacherous that the crew of every junk entering performed certain rites in the hope of warding off unfavourable influences.*

26
Whampoa, from Dane's Island

BEFORE the complete establishment of British naval and military superiority over the Chinese, the channel of Whampoa[1] was known only as the roadstead where foreign vessels, trading to Canton, were obliged to drop their anchors. In the passage up from Bocca Tigris, two bars are crossed; the second, near to the entrance — the first, immediately eastward of a group of islands, the principal of which are named by Europeans, French, Dane's and Whampoa.

French Island, westward of Dane's Island, forms the side scene of the illustration; it is one vast cemetery, divided impartially between the foreigner and the native, and occupied with the humble, low-lying tablet that records the early fall of the one, far from the place of his birth, as well as with the pompous, semicircular mausoleum which distinguishes, by its sweep and architecture, the rank and wealth of the other, whose pride lies humbled beneath it. To the left of the view is seen the entrance to the Tay-wang-kow passage, Junk river, which bounds Whampoa island, and separates it from Junk island.

The picturesque prospect which Whampoa and its encircling islets presents, has been the theatre of many military events. When the Modèste, a British frigate, was directed, during the late Chinese war, to pass Whampoa towards Canton, and subsequently the Sulphur was placed under similar orders, the opposition given by the battery at Howqua's Folly[2] at the north-west extremity of Whampoa island, and by Fort Napier,[3] which is directly opposite, was so contemptible that it is merely mentioned but not dwelt upon in the despatches. Howqua's Folly, built after Admiral Drury's expedition,[4] is a quadrangular structure, entirely of hewn granite, and mounting eight-and-twenty guns. Between these two forts, stakes were driven into the river-bed; and old junks were sunk, to obstruct the passage of the British; but the employment of war-steamers in the British navy since the previous visit of our ships to Whampoa, had escaped the knowledge of the Chinese, and gave to all their contrivances an appearance of extravagant folly.[5]

On a mound adjacent to the town, and near the western end of the island, the Whampoa pagoda rises to a height of one hundred and seventy feet; beyond the Junk river on the right, and on the point of Junk island, is another, inferior in gracefulness and height; and on the further bank of the Tay-wang-kow passage, a beautiful, light, and tapering temple stands conspicuously prominent. Canton-reach extends from Whampoa and French islands in a western direction, and is enclosed on the north by a range of lofty and rugged hills that form a delightful drooping distance.

---

[1] *Hwangpo until 1841 served as the port for Canton as far as foreign vessels were concerned — they were not allowed to proceed up the remaining five miles to the city. It continued to serve as a depot and dock for foreign merchant ships until 1877 when its facilities were purchased by the authorities at Canton (see map on p. 53)*

[2] *Named after Howqua, reputedly the richest merchant in China, if not the world; the senior member of the Co-hong during the period of the First Opium War, and highly respected amongst the foreign merchants. He was no doubt obliged to build this fort to demonstrate his patriotism.*

[3] *Lord Napier was the leader of an official British mission to enter into direct diplomatic relations with China in 1834, after the abolition of the East India Company's monopoly over the China trade. This episode was a major factor in the events leading to the clash between China and Britain five years later.*

[4] *Admiral Drury was the commander of the British forces that occupied Macao (to keep it from the French) during the Napoleonic Wars. He became involved in a quarrel with the Chinese authorities at Canton which led him to threaten the city with British warships.*

[5] *British steam warships played a decisive part in the First Opium War.*

27
Pagoda and Village on the Canal near Canton

ANIMATION increases as the city of Canton is approached, not solely from the cultivated character of the enclosing banks, the constant passing of vessels engaged in foreign trade, but more particularly from the vast amount of population permanently located on the watery surface. Pilot-houses, stores, merchants' villas, and groups of humble dwellings, overshadowed by waving pines, lend an air of cheerfulness to the ever-varying view; and, the style of architecture, combined with the seasonable decorations of the houses, add much agreeable effect to the moving picture. One locality is peculiarly gratifying from the liveliness of the scene, and assemblage of pleasing objects and circumstances. A row of picturesque cottages, on one bank, is approached from the water by a broad flight of steps, shaded in hot weather by the outspread branches of a lofty forest-tree; on the opposite bank stands a temple of Fo,[1] and a tall pagoda encircled by ramparts, where the Chinese sustained, for some twenty minutes, an attack from a small British force in the recent war with the empire. It is at this place, called the Yellow Pagoda, that so many junks stop, and their crews, disembarking, make offerings to the

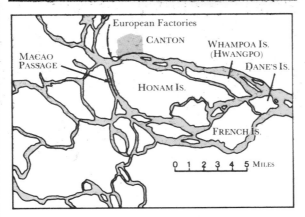

THE APPROACHES TO CANTON

tutelar deity of the islet for their safe return, or conciliate his favour for a prosperous voyage. From this venerated spot to the city-quays activity and, indeed, confusion, appear to increase with an accelerated speed, so that when once the noble panorama of the Yellow Pagoda, the majestic stream of the Cho-keang, and the distant amphitheatre of hills are passed, Honan and the sounds of the city-streets are soon encountered. This is the principal suburb allotted to foreigners for their residence, but the privilege is accompanied by so many infringements, that the value of the gift is much less than the giver could ever have contemplated. Every promenade is previously occupied by the most idle and ill-conducted of the native population, intermixed with a countless crowd of beggars. These troublesome characters hitherto, that is, previously to the Chinese war, with unblushing effrontery gathered around each foreigner, either to satiate vulgar curiosity, or extort, by pressing importunity, undue alms.

---

[1] *A Buddhist temple.*

A SUPPLEMENT OF COLOUR PLATES

CHINA AND BIRMAH

BRITISH FACTORIES, CANTON.

BAY OF BENGAL

CHINESE SOLDIERS.

HONG KONG.

SCALE.

Longitude East from Greenwich

The Illustrations by A.H. Wray, & Engraved by J.B. Allen.

The Map Drawn & Engraved by J. Rapkin.

THE LONDON PRINTING AND PUBLISHING COMPANY

Drawn by T. Allom.

Engraved by J. B. Allen.

The Emperor "Teaou-Kwang" reviewing his Guards, Palace of Peking.

Drawn by T. Allom.

Engraved by E. Brandard.

Western Gate, Peking.

Drawn by T. Allom.   Sketched on the spot by Captⁿ. Stoddart, R.N.   Engraved by S. Fisher.

Hong-Kong, from Kow-loon.

The Great Wall of China.

Drawn by T. Allom.

Engraved by T.A. Prior.

Cat Merchants and Tea Dealers at Tong-Chow.

(The Port of Peking)

Drawn by T. Allom.

Engraved by A. Willmore.

Kite-flying at Hae-kwan, on the Ninth Day of Ninth Moon.

28
The Grotto of Camöens, Macao

AMONGST the many interesting memorials in the vicinity of Macao, is the cave or grotto of Camöens, the most celebrated poet of the Portuguese. It is a rudely-constructed temple, standing on the brink of a precipice and commanding a most glorious prospect over the peninsula, and the sea that embraces it, and the mountains that rise rapidly on the opposite side of the roadstead. Visitors are led to the pleasure-grounds of a private seat, "the Casa,"[1] with no inconsiderable degree of pride and thence to the little pavilion on the rock, where a bust of the poet is preserved. The son of a ship-captain, and born at Lisbon about the year 1524, he was placed at the college of Coimbra; from which he returned, after passing the required time, to his native city. Here he fell passionately in love with a lady of the palace, Catherine d'Attayde, and was banished to Santarem, as the result of a dispute in which his luckless attachment had involved him. Despair preying on a mind so sensitive, he now became a soldier, and serving in the expedition which the Portuguese sent against Morocco, he composed poetry in the midst of battles. Danger kindled genius — genius animated courage. An arrow having deprived him of his right eye at the siege of Ceuta, he hoped that his wounds would receive a recompense which was denied to his talents; but in this expectation also he was disappointed, solely as the result of the envy of others. Filled with indignation at this studied neglect, he embarked for India in the year 1553, and landed at Goa, near to the spot where his father perished by shipwreck only three years after. At first he was incited to deeds of glory by the example of his countrymen in India, and exercised his powerful imagination in celebrating their praise in a lengthened epic poem. However, finally disgusted with many acts of cruelty and perfidy in the government of India, he wrote a satire upon the authors, which caused his banishment to the settlement of Macao. His appointment of judge at this place was but an honourable name for exile; but here leisure was found at length for the realization of his great visions and, selecting Vasco de Gama's Indian expedition as the subject, Camöens devoted the palmy years of his life to the composition of the "Lusiad."

Sailing once more for Europe, the destiny of Camöens followed him, and at the mouth of the river Mekong in Cochin-China, he suffered shipwreck, the only treasure which he saved being the MS. of his poem. Reaching Goa after this narrow escape from a watery grave, new griefs awaited him: and here he encountered renewed persecutions, being imprisoned for debt, and only released on the responsibility of his friends. On being set free once more, Camöens was encouraged by the patronage of royalty; the youthful monarch, Sebastian, manifesting an admiration of his poems, and taking an interest in the poet. However, on an expedition against the Moors in Africa, Sebastian fell in the battle before the city of Alcacar, in 1578; and Camöens, in losing his prince, lost everything. Returning to his native country, friendless, impoverished, envied, he yet wrote lyric poems, some of which contain the most moving complaints of the neglect of literary worth, and the ingratitude of mankind to public benefactors.

Finally, being no longer able to provide for himself or relieve his infirmities, he obtained admission into the chief hospital of Lisbon; and there, this great ornament of his country miserably expired in the sixty-second year of his age. Fifteen years afterwards, a splendid monument was erected to his memory; and his works have since been translated into every European language.

---

[1] *The founder of the house and estate of La Casa is not known. At one stage it belonged to the Jesuits, and at the start of the nineteenth century was being rented by a wealthy British merchant. It later reverted to Portuguese ownership.*

THE island of Hong-Kong, is separated from the mainland by a strait not more than half a mile in width in some places, but in others extending to five. The Peninsula of Kow-loon forms the opposite shore; and on its extreme point, and directly commanding the entrance to the English town, which has grown up there with almost miraculous rapidity, stood two Chinese forts. As the bay of Hong-Kong is one of the most admirable in the Eastern seas, it is an object of the utmost consequence that it should be protected from the attacks of the Chinese. Its natural advantages consist in depth and capaciousness, as well as in the safe anchorage it affords to the largest vessels riding at a cable-length from the shore, during the typhoons by which the Chinese seas are agitated. The lofty mountain that rises in the back-ground of the accompanying view, and seems to impend over the waters of the strait, is called the Peak of Hong-Kong; and, although beautiful in the distance from its form and outline, it is sterile and unpromising upon more close examination. Its summit and projecting points are of hard granite, a most valuable acquisition to the settlers, as being a durable and accommodating material for building; and, as in all regions of similar structure, the granite is found in the highest position, here it attains an elevation of two thousand feet above the level of the sea.

On the arrival of our expedition in these waters, in 1842, the fleet procured supplies at Kow-loon, where they found an active trade, but to a small extent, conducted by the natives. After the first

29
Fort Victoria, Kow-loon

compact into which we entered with the Chinese authorities it was agreed that the peninsula of Kow-loon should be considered neutral ground, and that the two batteries which stood there should be dismantled, to remove all apprehension on our part. The Chinese have been known to observe their engagements, but in this instance they were resentful of our recent successes. However, to their promises we trusted, and, leaving Kow-loon in their custody, believed ourselves secure from insult or aggression at Hong-Kong.

Scarcely had we indulged in a cessation from active war, when the imperial government expressed its total disregard for treaties, especially with Barbarians, and without hesitation resumed an aggressive attitude. This iniquitous measure decided the question of occupancy at Kow-loon; and, instead of the old battery, whose useless and time-worn artillery was quite in character with their artillery-men, a reconstruction, but in the Chinese architectural manner, has taken place; and a stout fortress, manned by brave British military, has succeeded, known by the appropriate, and now ever-memorable name in China, of *Fort Victoria*.[1]

---

[1] *Before the British occupation of Hong Kong, there were two Chinese forts sited at the tip of Tsim Sha Tsui. They were seized during the course of 1841 in consequence of the breakdown of the Convention of Chuenpi and of an altercation between Captain Elliott and the Canton authorities over the supposed neutrality of the Kowloon Peninsula. One of them was then named Fort Victoria.*

IV CHINESE OCCUPATIONS

In a celebrated passage from the rescript of the Ch'ien-lung Emperor to Lord Macartney in 1793, the Emperor declared:

'Our Celestial Empire possesses all things in prolific abundance and lacks no product within its borders. There is, therefore, no need to import the manufactures of outside barbarians in exchange for our own products, but the tea and porcelain which the Celestial Empire produces are absolute necessities to European nations.'

The Emperor may have overestimated the part played by tea and porcelain in the economies of the West (although tea was a major concern of the London merchants), but what he had to say about the self-sufficiency of his empire was, in the circumstances, substantially correct. Apart from the tea, which accounted for ninety-five per cent of British imports from China, raw silk, rhubarb and porcelain — all of which the Chinese were convinced were indispensable to the foreigners — formed the main British purchases, while to India flowed nankeen silks, alum, pepper, sugar, vermilion and chinaware. The balance of trade was in favour of China until it was discovered by the Westerners that opium could replace silver as payment for Chinese goods.

The main tea-producing areas were the provinces of Fukien, Anhwei and Kiangsi. Mulberry for silkworms was cultivated in Szechuan, Kweichow, Kiangsi and Chekiang, while the silk-weaving industry was centred at Nanking, Soochow, Hangchow and Huchow. The greatest centre for porcelain wares was at Ching-te Chen (in Kiangsi), with two to three hundred kilns employing hundreds of thousands of workers, before its destruction at the hands of the Taiping rebels. A considerable section of the population was engaged in trade and business in one form or the other, as is demonstrated in some of the following plates which speak for themselves. However, the bulk of the population (eighty per cent.) were tillers of the soil, primarily engaged in growing the empire's staple food, rice. Western observers had an axe to grind whenever they passed comment on the Chinese scene, but there can be little doubt that for the great masses of the inhabitants of nineteenth century China, life was brutal, nasty and short.

30 Rice-sellers at Tong-chang-foo

SUCH scenes as this party of rice-eaters presents are frequently witnessed by travellers, more particularly along the line of the Imperial canal, on which Tong-chang-foo is situated. The military station rendering a halt for the payment of taxes necessary, the barge-pullers seize the opportunity to rest and refresh themselves. A guard of military-police being paraded, during the settlement of the dues by the task-master or slave-driver, the pullers seat themselves beneath an immense umbrella supported by a bamboo pillar, and are supplied by the landlady of this very primitive and very picturesque "inn", with bowls, chopsticks, and all other requisites for the occasion. Assembled round an earthen stove, at which the rice-meal, mixed with vegetables and fried in rancid oil or animal offal, is dressed, and disengaging themselves from their cumbrous bamboo hats, some also twisting the long queue, round their heads, they raise the bowl to the edge of the lower lip, against which they press it closely, and, with the chopsticks throw in their food expeditiously, conveniently, and with an astonishing degree of cleanliness. In China, as well as in Western Europe, the pipe forms a necessary part of the labourer's personal property; and, from the great length of this instrument amongst Orientals when inserted in the pocket a very considerable portion always protrudes. As stations may not occur at those intervals of time or space best suited to the pullers' needs, it is his wise practice to carry a supply of meal in a pouch suspended at his side, along with a hard wooden flat spoon, such as the hostess of the great umbrella is employing besides his accustomed chopsticks. On the ground, and close by the figure in the act of placing the chopsticks in his mouth, lie several flat boards with cords passed through them; these are the harness, or gear, which the puller applies to his breast, to save it from the effects of too great pressure, in carrying out his onerous task.

31
Feeding Silkworms and Sorting the Cocoons

HAVING destroyed the chrysalides, and wound off the produce in its primitive state, from the cocoons destined for reefing, the mere husbandry of silk gathering is concluded. And so short is the period, in France only six weeks, consumed in this species of culture, that no harvest yields a return of greater celerity and certainty. In a country where trade is conducted, not by companies, or associations, or partnerships, but by individual exertion, the culture and produce of silk are peculiarly suitable, as affording a means of employing small capital with every prospect of early revenue. Females devote much of their time and their talents to this occupation; they are either engaged in feeding and rearing the worms or winding off the cocoons. Sometimes the patriarch of the family purchases cocoons, by which the risk of rearing is avoided, and fills up his daughter's leisure time with the process of filature. There are,

of course, some nurseries or factories, where silk is prepared expressly for exportation, but in general the manufacture is for home-consumption. The Chinese dislike foreigners, from practice and national institutes, therefore less attention is paid to objects of external commerce here than in other countries; besides, all kinds of trade are held in very low estimation in China, as they were of old in Athens and in Rome.

Around a pool, of a foot or two in depth, sheds or open corridors are arranged, appropriated to different parts of the process of cleaning and preparing the floretta for market. Beneath one series are the females employed in the less laborious duty of reeling the raw silk. From the reelers' verandas, the material is consigned to those of the washers, and dyers, and bleachers, successively.

32
Loading Tea-junks at Tseen-tang

ON a tributary to the river of "the Nine Bends,"[1] and in the province of Fokien, is a romantic, rich, and remarkable spot, the resort of tea-factors, and the principal loading-place, in the district, for tea destined for the Canton and other markets. The hills and the valleys here are equally favourable to the production of this staple of China, and the tea-tree itself has been carefully examined, and its peculiarities ascertained by Europeans in this locality, with more minuteness and care than elsewhere.

Tea-plants are grown in rows about five feet apart, the intermediate furrows being kept free from weeds, and insects; and the trees are not allowed to attain a height inconvenient for pickers. Indeed, when the tea-tree reaches its eighth year, it is removed, to make way for a more youthful successor, the produce of old trees being unfit for use. The flowers of the tree, which are white, and resemble the common monthly-rose in form, are succeeded by soft green berries or pods, each enclosing from one to three white seeds. March is the first month in the year for picking, both as to time and quality, and great precautions are observed in this ceremony. The pickers are required to prepare themselves for their task by a specific process. For several weeks previous to the harvest, they take such diet only as may communicate agreeable odours to the skin and breath, and, while gathering, they wear gloves of perfumed leather. Every leaf is plucked separately, but, as practice confers perfection, an expert performer will gather twelve pounds in the course of a day. April is the second season; — leaves gathered in this month afford a coarser and inferior description of tea; they are plucked with fewer ceremonies than those of the preceding crop, but, should a large proportion of small and delicate leaves appear, these are selected, and sold as the produce of the first picking. In May and June inferior kinds are gathered, and even sometimes later. Leaves of the earliest crop are of small size, of delicate colour and aromatic flavour, with little fibre and little bitterness; those of the second picking are of a dull green; and the last gatherings are characterized by a still darker shade of the same colour, and a much coarser grain. Quality is influenced by the age of the plantation, by the degree of exposure to which the tree has been accustomed, by the nature of the soil, and the skill of the cultivator.

An obvious distinction exists between the farmer, or grower, and the manufacturer: the former separates the respective qualities with the utmost care, and disposes of them, in that selected manner, to the manufacturer, either at his own house, or in the most convenient market; the latter removes his purchases to his private factory, and there, taking certain measures from each heap, mixes them together, in proportions producing the exact quality he wishes to give each particular class, or number of chests; the farmer therefore is a separator — the manufacturer, a concentrator. And now the process of planting, rearing, gathering, drying, separating, and mixing being completed, it only remains to pack the preparation into chests, and tread it down sufficiently; in this convenient form it is put on board the junks at Tseen-tang, and other loading-places in the tea-growing countries, and carried to the stores at Canton or Macao.

---

[1] *The Chiu-long Kiang which flows into the sea at Amoy.*

33
Transplanting Rice

RICE-grounds consist of neatly enclosed spaces, the clay banks surrounding them seldom exceeding two feet in height. The primary operation of tillage-ploughing is performed with a very primitive implement, that consists of a beam, handle, and cutting blade. The buffalo, or water-ox, is then called in, to draw the three-barred harrow with wooden teeth over the surface, after which the earth is deemed sufficiently pulverized to receive the seed. Having been steeped in a liquid preparation to accelerate germination, and avert the attacks of insects, the seed is sown, very thickly, and, almost immediately after, a thin sheet of water is induced over the enclosure. After the interval of a few days only, the shoots overtop the water, and this is the signal for transplanting, which consists in plucking up the plants by the roots, cutting off the tops of the blades, and setting each root separately. The last process is aided either by turning furrows with the plough, or opening holes with the dibble. With such rapidity is transplanting performed by the experienced, that with ordinary exertion five-and-twenty plants may be carefully set in a minute. The harrow having pulverized in the first instance, and subsequently diffused the seeds more equally, the hoe is frequently employed to clear between the plants.

Each rice-field being partitioned into many minor enclosures, it is simple to conduct a rivulet into any particular plantation, through an opening in the clay ridge that surrounds it. Sometimes a natural brook contributes a sufficient supply, but more frequently the labour of the peasant provides it. Chain-pumps, with their lines of buckets, are

in common use; a series of flat boards, exactly fitted to the channel through which it is to be forced, confines the water between each pair, forming extemporary buckets. These are worked by a foot-mill of proportionate dimensions; but labour still more intense is dedicated to this necessary operation, irrigating rice-grounds. In one of the most intensive stages, two men stand opposite to each other on projecting banks of a stream, holding ropes

securely attached to a bucket, which is filled by relaxing, and raised by tightening the cords, then by a skilful jerk they empty the contents into a reservoir, or throw it in the direction of the conduit cut for the irrigation of some one field. Another contrivance for the same purpose consists of a long pole, unequally divided in its length, and made to turn on a pivot across an upright post. A bucket attached to the shorter arm of this lever is easily lowered into the water, and, when filled, by the application of a small power at the extremity of the longer arm, it is soon raised, and discharged into the reservoir.

Irrigation having performed its anticipated work, the rice begins to grow with rapidity. As the crop approaches to maturity, the sluices are closed, the waters withheld, and soon the yellow tinge of the ripening grain invites the reaper's toil. With a sickle similar to our common serrated reaping-hook, the crop is soon prostrated, on a surface, now rendered perfectly dry by evaporation and absorption; after which the bundles are removed, in frames suspended at the extremities of a bamboo pole, the national mode of portage, to the threshing apparatus, of whatever kind it may be. In May or June the first crop is generally cut, and before the harvesting is wholly completed, preparations are begun for a new or second sowing. The second crop attains maturity in October or November, but the second stubble, instead of being burned, is turned under by the plough, left to decompose in the earth, and become manure for the spring-crop of the following year.

34
The Kilns at King-tan[1]

THE limestone district of King-tan, being visited not only by travellers in passenger barges, but also by trading junks, presents more frequent examples of the despotism of this great empire than most other localities. In view of its huge population, the employment of human labour or animal power for every task can be understood, but even this is insufficient to justify the cruelty exercised over the tribe of pullers. Descending from the mountains, where the soil denies support to the majority of those that first drew breath amidst their summits, a robust and hardy set of men undertake the toilsome life of the puller (tseen-foo). Half naked, and furnished with a description of gear, consisting of a breast-board, or sometimes a cushioned wooden bar, to the ends of which the ropes are attached, a number of men, according to the weight of the junk, is harnessed to the work of pulling against the stream. Their attitude and efforts are fully expressed in the illustration, where they appear not merely to give their muscular power, but their corporal weight, to strain the chief rope that is tied around the mast-head. Engaged for sixteen successive hours, during which no space for refreshment is allowed, time being an object of his merciless employer, he is kept unflinchingly to his work by an overseer supplied with a long bamboo.

This humble application of human power is rendered still more humiliating from the cruelty and despotism exercised by government to obtain the pullers on any emergency. A Tartar corps is despatched to scour the country through which the imperial junks are about to pass, and press into the service all ages without distinction. It is in vain that parents plead the tender age of their offspring, or their own declining years, and father,

husband, sons, are indiscriminately enrolled by force into the service of the state. To prevent desertion, the impressed men are driven into an adjoining temple, or station-house, and there confined, sometimes for days, until the arrival of the junks, and of the pullers whom they are destined to succeed. A foreman now undertakes their management, and plies his long bamboo, emboldened by the confidence which a Tartar troop inspires. Pullers in government-service undergo the most distressing fatigue; sometimes they have to wade through mire that comes up to their very arms, at others to swim across creeks and rivulets, and immediately after expose their naked and exhausted bodies to the painful influence of a burning sun. Resistance is met by the lash, or by the punishment of face-slapping; — obedience, by wages of one shilling[2] a day, without any consideration of the time that will be occupied in the return of those ill-used beings to their families and homes.

Much has been said about the pullers' song. It is a mournful sound, that summons each brother of the trade to alleviate the burden of his neighbour by pulling in due time. There is neither harmony nor cheerfulness in the poor Chinaman's chorus of *Wo-to-hei-o*, in which the saddest letter of the alphabet predominates.

---

[1] *As becomes apparent on reading the description above, the appropriate title would have been 'The Barge-Pullers'. It was conditions such as those described here which gave Westerners their sense of superiority in confronting the Chinese Empire, and enabled them to forget their own forms of human exploitation.*

[2] *It is obviously impossible to compute what value the shilling had in this context, but the inference that it represented a mere pittance is clear.*

35
An Itinerant
Doctor at Tien-sing[1]

OF all that tribe of impostors, which, as a plague, infests society here, the quack doctor is one of the most knavish, and most popular: his theme appealing to the personal interest of every individual, many who openly condemn, secretly encourage his frauds, by purchasing his cures, and submitting to his coarse remedies. Provided with a regular bench or counter, he spreads on this his various packets, jars, images, instruments, and pitch-plasters, interspersed with scrolls of paper, on which, like our European quacks, the number of wonderful cures effected by his medicines, with the names of those that were healed by them, are emblazoned in letters of gold. Oratorical skill, or rather great conversational powers, constitute a chief qualification in a Chinese doctor, whose cures are accomplished as much by persuasion on his part, as credulity on that of the patient. There is not a malady in the long list of sorrows to which flesh is heir — there is not a deformity to which the human frame can be reduced by accident or birth which the Chinese quack has not the hardihood to undertake relieving. The lame, blind, and deaf, are generally assembled in numbers around the impostor's stand, although no knowledge from experience has led them to repose confidence in his healing powers; their hopes being built on his eloquent account of his own abilities, aided by that inclination to trust, which everywhere characterizes the weak, the sick, and the ignorant.

Behind a counter, (in the Illustration) is seen an itinerant doctor, dilating on the virtues of a anti-

dote against the bite of serpents; one of his assistants is actually putting the head of the *cobra capella*, or hooded snake, into his mouth, while a less intrepid, but equally useful assistant, is exchanging the miraculous drug for *cash* or *tseen*. The great impostor himself, mounted on a stool, his head protected by a conical hat of split bamboo, a cloak of thick, coarse, compact cloth enclosing his arms, and a similar covering being secured around his waist by a silken girdle, holds a serpent in one hand, and the antidote to its venomous bite in the other.

So well-trained is this mischievous reptile, that it tries to bite its owner, and submits to disappointment with the appearance of reluctance. Having proved that this particular enemy of mankind still retains its will to injure in the most convincing manner, and requires to be guarded against with caution, the doctor takes a medicated ball from one of the packets with which the counter is strewn, and, when the snake renews its attempts, presents the ball to it, upon which it instantly recoils, and endeavours to escape from his grasp. Should this demonstration be insufficient, the efficacy of the charm is still more convincingly established by merely rubbing the forehead, cheek, hand, or any other unprotected part with the antidote, and presenting it to the reptile, which appears to retreat with the same dislike and precipitation, as when the entire ball was shown to it.

---

[1] *Tientsin.*

36
Cat Merchants and Tea Dealers at Tong-chow[1]

IN China the voracity of the people is everywhere apparent; every object of industry or occupation seems to have as its object the appeasing of appetite. The rich and elevated are decided gourmets; the middle and lower classes as decided sensualists. The tastes of the one are scarcely limited by the extent of their revenues, the voracity of the other unrestricted by the most unusual species of food. Being the most omnivorous people in the world, there is not an animal or plant that can be procured by art and industry, and eaten without risk of life, that is not pressed into the service by these gastronomers: the flesh of wild horses is highly prized, the larvæ of the sphinx-moth, bears' paws, and the feet of other animals brought from Tartary, Cambodia and Siam, are deemed delicious; and edible birds'-nests are esteemed at the banquets of the mandarins, for which they are occasionally made into a soup. At Tong-chow, to which the stewards of the noble families of Peking repair to purchase meats for their lords, the salesmen enter the market-place, or step from their junks upon shore, having baskets suspended at the extremities of a carrying-pole, in which are contained dogs, cats, rats, or birds, either tame or wild, generally alive — sea-slugs, and grubs found in the sugar-cane. The species of dog most in request is a small spaniel; the poor animals appear particularly dejected in their imprisonment, not even looking up in the hope of freedom; whilst the cats, on the contrary, maintain an incessant squalling, and seem never to despair of escaping from a fate which otherwise must prove inevitable. In the ancient Chinese writings, cats are spoken of as a delicacy at table; but the species alluded to was found wild in Tartary, and brought thence into China, where they were regularly fed for the markets of the principal cities.

As far as appearance is concerned, rats, when butchered, for they are not brought to market alive, are by no means disgusting. They are neatly prepared, slit down the breast, and hung in rows from the carrying-poles by skewers passed through their distended hind-legs.

In the immediate vicinity of the wharfs, or horses' heads, the accustomed name for landing-places or jetties amongst the Chinese, at Tong-chow, are stalls where refreshments are sold to the boatmen and loungers; tea, however, is the universal beverage; and the vender, standing beneath a canopy of sail-cloth, made of the fibre of the bamboo, and supported by bamboo canes, invites all passers-by to taste the favourite refreshment. Cups, much inferior in capacity to those in general use amongst us, are laid with regularity along a marble counter, at the end of which stands a stove and boiler, where the tea is prepared and kept warm. The scene around presents an extraordinary instance of the universal application of the bamboo. Beside the tarpaulin supporters, table-frame, and trellis-work of the tea-vender's shop, the conical baskets in which the cats are brought to market, the pole from which they are suspended, the broad-leafed hat of the cat-merchant, the walking-stick of the buyer, the masts, sails, ropes, of the trading junks which lie close to the shore, as well as the frame-work and sail-cloths that sustain and form an awning, are all obtained or manufactured from this invaluable cane.

---

[1] *Tungchow, a once important staging point, and, later on, railway junction on the main route from Tientsin to Peking, 15 miles from the capital.*

37
Cap-vender's Shop, Canton

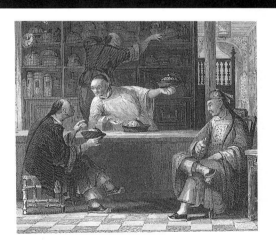

A CAP-VENDER'S establishment is not infrequently a scene of gossiping, — a fashionable lounge, a rendezvous of those whose badge is idleness. Open in front, it is decorated with lanterns, and emblems of trade, and inscriptions, the latter setting forth the integrity of the long line of occupants, the quality of goods exclusively issued from that store, the reasonable charges uniformly made, and the total impossibility of trusting to the honour of humanity under certain circumstances. All these sentiments are expressed in characters of gold, on tablets suspended at the side of the open casement. A little railing, partly for protection, but chiefly for ornament and architectural finish, runs along the external edge of the counter, and within it are stands supporting specimen or pattern caps, a practice adopted with ingenuity and taste by the hat and bonnet venders in London and in Paris. Entrance to the shop is often interrupted by a begging priest,[1] in a humiliating posture, endeavouring to attract attention by the gentle humming of a familiar hymn, accompanied with the more annoying tap of a small ivory pick upon a piece of hollowed wood, in shape resembling a pear.

As the illustration represents a well-known and respectable store in Canton, the style of decoration, attendance, and fitting-up, may be taken as a sample of its class. The goods manufactured and sold here are intended for the wealthy part of the community only, of whom the cap appears to be a special prerogative.

Should the season prove intensely sultry, the tapering queue[2] alone adorns the aristocrat's head; in less warm weather a skull-cap of padded silk is worn; and in still colder, a cap made of the thinnest rattan, slightly woven, having the edge turned up all round. These different styles are adapted to summer and winter, to home and out-of-door use. The summer cap most generally worn is a hollow upright cone of bamboo filaments, the apex of which is terminated by a red, blue, white, or gilded ball, or by an opaque button, according to the rank of the wearer. A large lock of red hair, taken from the abdomen of the water-ox, flows from the insertion of the button into the apex; and sometimes a beautiful agate, a lapis lazuli, or gem called yû, sparkles in the frontal border. In winter, the cone is exchanged for a covering of more solid manufacture and more appropriate shape. It is the cap with the turned-up edge. The rattan is more firmly woven in this than in the summer caps, but the ornaments, the button of distinction, and the tuft of hair, are the same as before. At this season, too, especially in the northern provinces, the skull-cap is worn much within doors, and the bamboo out of doors. Almost all the social habits of this ancient people are regulated by imperial decrees, issued arbitrarily at various times, and amongst them are rules for the proper, rational, and becoming attire of the individual. These laws provide for the change of the summer for the winter head-dress, and *vice versâ;* and a broad hint is given to society by the example of the chief mandarin, or magistrate, of every district, as well as by an announcement in the imperial gazette, that the period has arrived when this part of the national costume *must* undergo the change prescribed by the law.

[1] *A Buddhist priest, the giving of alms to whom constituted an act of merit.*

[2] *The queue or pigtail worn by the all male Chinese was mandatory under Manchu rule, as a sign of Chinese subjection. Its use was prohibited after the Revolution of 1911.*

ONE custom peculiar to China is the practice of carrying lanterns. Every pedestrian in the streets, on the roads, or any other public avenue, is required, after nightfall, to carry a lantern, on which his name and residence are painted; and a violation of the law subjects the offender to arrest by the police, and imprisonment until the mandarin's leisure allows him to hear and condemn him. Every vehicle in the highways is obliged to set up a national lamp, and the river-surface at Canton, and other cities similarly seated, presents a continuous sheet of light, or fire, from the reflection of the lamps which all boats hang out at dusk.

Both the shape and material of which lanterns are formed, differ considerably. Every mathematical figure — the sphere, square, pentagon, hexagon, and many others, with a considerable number of sides — is enlisted in their manufacture; the frames may be of wood, ivory, or metal, and the designs and patterns of the most costly evince a very accomplished and practised taste in what is generally styled scroll-work. Glass is rarely used in lanterns, or indeed for any other purpose than as mirrors, but the number of substitutes is endless. Amongst them are to be reckoned horn, silk, oyster-shells, paper, thread-netting or gauze, the latter coated with a tenacious varnish made from the *gigartina tenax*, a kind of seaweed found in the Indian archipelago.

38
Show-room of a Lantern Merchant at Peking

The manufacture of lanterns is of course a profitable business, and it is difficult to determine to which part in the process the greater share of admiration belongs — the size and perfection of the horn, which is made with a simple pair of pincers, an iron boiler, and a small stove; or the richly-painted and embroidered panes that fill the framework. A lantern-painter is an artist of no mean rank: he possesses a very extensive knowledge of design, and is a master of colouring. None but the most agreeable subjects, whether landscape or figure, and the most gaudy colours, are considered appropriate on the panes or the panels of a lantern. And this is the uniform sentiment, although the ornament may be intended to light a hall of Confucius, or a temple of idolatry.

A lantern merchant's show-room is a fashionable lounge: and, as there is no limit to the number of these articles with which an apartment of ceremony may be adorned; save its capacity only, a continual business appears to be going on, and rivalship amongst this class of decorators is for ever active. The patterns painted on the lantern-panes vary with the season, like those of silk and cotton manufactures in Europe; and, it is only an act of domestic duty on the mandarin's part to visit the show-rooms at the proper period, select the newest pattern, and purchase it for the apartments of his wife and daughters.

V
CHINESE RELIGIOUS FESTIVALS

Chinese religion, not surprisingly, is totally different in concept and approach to the beliefs cherished in the West, and therefore to most Westerners, almost totally incomprehensible. In the eyes of the Roman Catholic and Protestant missionaries who flocked into China after the Opium Wars, Chinese religion and its practice were regarded as little more than a complicated mumbo-jumbo of superstition and idolatry. Although such an observation might have held truth for religion at the popular level – and one must remember there were over 450 million souls in China in the 1850s — it was certainly not valid as far as educated and thinking Chinese were concerned. In fact the boundary between religion and philosophy in China was always somewhat tenuous, and in many respects the three major 'religions' which the Chinese were supposed to profess (and many Chinese professed all three, to add further to the general European confusion over the matter) merely expressed or interpreted certain basic concepts which dominated all Chinese thinking.

First amongst these concepts was that of a universal order which embraced all things and in which, in stark contrast to Western beliefs, Man was not the central figure. The nature of the universe and of its Creator were there but only in vague outline; they were not clearly defined or personalized. Related to this basic idea was the identification of ethics and morality with the natural order of things, with which one ought to try and conform; the placing of social values before individual ones; a belief in the essential duality of nature (the yang and yin — for example, male and female, light and dark, sun and moon) and the existence of certain forces (kuei — evil spirits, and feng-shui — forces of nature) that could influence and be influenced for good or bad.

In terms of organized beliefs or ideas, Confucianism led the way partly because it enjoyed the direct patronage of the state, especially in Manchu times, and because its teachings formed the basis of the syllabus for the civil service examinations. In seeking conformity with the Universal Order, the Confucianists stressed the importance of tradition in society and the need to adhere to that tradition by maintaining time-honoured rituals. Proper observances were the basis of good conduct, and society was secure provided the ruler set a good example. The philosophical features of Confucianism were reinforced by its adoption and encouragement of the animistic tradition of ancestor-worship. Taoism placed its emphasis on the mystical aspects of the universe and developed an outlook and philosophy which encouraged passivity and withdrawal from life. This might have proved its undoing if the arrival of Buddhism in China had not provided it with a model for more practical organization. Taoist temples and priests proliferated after the spread of Buddhism. Buddhism first penetrated China around the first century AD but made its major impact about six centuries later. It fitted in well with the prevalent Chinese world view, and in China assimilated much of the Chinese outlook.

The Chinese, therefore, were not fanatics in their religion, and could receive, side by side, different interpretations of the universe. At the same time, popular beliefs could also flourish alongside the three major ways of thought, forming part and parcel of Chinese values and outlook. All to the greater confusion of the foreigner!

39
Propitiatory Offerings for Departed Relatives

IT is probable that the most educated Europeans who have hitherto travelled in China have failed to understand properly the rites and ceremonies of the people. Hence it is, that when access is permitted to the halls, and temples, and public places of China, we meet at every step with some new object of surprise.

In the extraordinary ceremonies related to the memory of the departed is implied something more than obtaining a passport to the seats of the blessed for the departed relative or friend. They dread his reappearance on earth in ghostly form, to terrify, if not avenge, the injuries done to him in life. The visitors of the lower regions are supposed to return to this upper world on the first day of the Seventh Moon, which falls some time in the month of August, and this event is commemorated by offerings and prayers, made before special altars, to avert the anger of the spirits, or to influence the fortunes of the devotees in a favourable manner. A temporary temple being erected for the occasion, its walls are hung with poorly-designed, and badly painted, representations of the tortures to which the wicked are exposed. Numerous altars are raised to the spirits of the dead, decked with every species of ornament which the resources of the suppliant can afford. Priests are present to direct the prayer and to perform a particular request before the altar that may be made. His next duty is to chant a sort of requiem for the souls of the departed. Food, including substantial and delicate dishes, is also offered in profusion, along with quantities of coloured paper, representing clothes, all of which it is imagined the spirits require in their abodes. At the close, however, of this solemn ceremony the garments are thrown into the flames of the stove that stands in the temple — the food consigned to the stomachs of the priests — and the devotees return to their homes in tumult.

40
A Devotee
Consulting the
Sticks of Fate

IN every situation, public or private, where the three ways meet in any city, town, village, on the summits of the highest mountains, in the recesses of the deepest vales, in the most unfrequented solitudes, in the lonely shelter of almost impenetrable forests, in situations as opposite as the passions of one human heart to those of another, temples of fortune or fate are erected, the doors of which stand open for ever, inviting the passerby to enter, and learn his fortune. Here an altar is raised to this most capricious and purblind goddess of chance on which vases are arranged, containing flattened pieces of wood resembling the leaves of a Chinese MS. book, or the spatula of a chemist. On these, which are called the Sticks of Fate, certain words are inscribed, having a mysterious connection with each other, and with the contents of a library of oracles, kept in the temple for reference and consultation.

In those out-of-the-way places where the scarcity of visitors would render the livelihood of a priest dependent upon their bounty precarious, the temple is untenanted; the Sticks stand in their urn, protected by superstition only; and the book of fate is chained to the pillars of the altar. In great thoroughfares there is always an attendant priest, a large supply of books of reference, and hideous figures, allegorical of the darkness that interrupts our view into futurity. Occasions of applying to the Sticks of Fate, are sometimes of moment; such as undertaking a journey, building a house, purchasing a new wife, or burying a deceased relation. The devotee, having paid the priest in advance, takes up the vase, and continues to shake it with becoming timidity until a pair of Sticks falls out. The priest then examines the inscriptions, and, comparing them with the pages, or paragraphs, or number, in the volume of oracles, declares whether the applicant is likely to succeed in his undertaking. Indefatigable in meeting all the demands of worldly industry, the Chinaman is reluctant to obey even that very deity whose aid he solicits; and, should a first or a second throw fail to afford that entire satisfaction which he anticipated, he perseveres until conquered fortune yields the victory. The purity of his gratitude is now displayed by the clear flame of a pile which he immediately kindles, throwing into it pieces of paper, covered with tinfoil;[1] and it is in these ceremonies that the greatest portion of the tinfoil imported into China from Europe is consumed.

---

[1] *In fact, the main market for tin from South-East Asia prior to the rise of its demand by Western industry in the nineteenth century was China, for the purposes described above.*

41
Ceremony of "Meeting the Spring"

NATIONAL amusements amongst the Chinese are generally associated with sanctity and every cardinal event in earthly affairs is referred to some revolution of the heavenly bodies — some phenomenon in the skies — some periodic change in the great government of the universe. They pay much attention to the solar and lunar motions, and are zealous in their celebration of festivities in honour of both. When the sun is in the fifteenth of Aquarius, and when the second February moon appears, it is the custom to form a procession, and go forth to meet the coming spring. Before, however, the festal day arrives, the more pious visit the various temples of Fo, or of Taou, or the Hall of Confucius,[1] or those dedicated to eminent men of times passed by. Those less infected with superstitious enthusiasm, take advantage of the prevailing idleness, and pay periodical visits to their friends and relations in distant provinces, or make parties of pleasure to favourite places of recreation. A third class, however, uniting the extremes of riot and religion, devote their leisure to the joyous celebration of the approaching season. A decade of days is appropriated to the ceremonies specified, and distinguished by the object of worship on each day respectively. The fowl, dog, pig, sheep, ox, horse, man, grain, hemp, and pea, are the natural products that constitute the subject of procession and veneration successively. Two of the ten days are held in greater reverence than the rest; these are the festivals of man and of the buffalo. On the latter occasion, a procession, formed at an agreed rendez-vous, advances to some rural temple, where it is received by the chief magistrate of the district, who offers a traditional sacrifice, and prostrates himself before the symbols of the season, borne by the procession-bearers. All those taking part are decorated with ribands or garlands; some are supplied with instruments of music, such as drums, gongs, horns; others carry banners, lanterns, or representations of pine-apples, and fruits of larger growth. Boys, dressed like carnival spirits, and seated on rustic altars, or on the branches of trees, are carried along in litters; on other stages are arranged little maids, dressed to represent the tea-plant, the usefulness of the leaf and the beauty of the blossom being meant to express the distinguishing characters of the softer sex. Above all, rises a huge buffalo, or water-ox, made of clay, or of a bamboo frame-work, covered with paper, and borne by a number of able-bodied worshippers, dressed in spring colours. It is not unusual to have a hundred tables, or litters, in a procession, each sustaining a number of boys or girls, an effigy of the water-ox, or of the human face divine. Arriving at the door of an appointed temple, the che-foo,[2] who had been in waiting there from the preceding day, advances to welcome them, in his capacity of Priest of Spring. He is *pro tempore* the highest officer in the district, exacting obedience from the viceroy, should they meet, during his ten days' sovereignty. Gorgeously attired, and shaded beneath an umbrella of state, enriched with embroidery, he delivers a speech in praise of spring, and recommends the virtues of agriculture; after which he strikes the figure of the water-ox three times with a whip, as the commencement of the ploughing season. This is the signal for general action; the crowd now proceed to stone the buffalo, from which, as it tumbles to pieces, numbers of little images fall out, for which a general scramble takes place. Proceeding to the various public offices, the cortège halts in front of each, and there makes a noisy demonstration, in return for the images, or medals, so generously thrown amongst them by the authorities.

---

[1] *The temples of the three main religions, Buddhism (Fo), Taoism and Confucianism.*

[2] *Che-foo* (chih-fu/zhifu) – *the prefect, the official in charge of a prefecture* (fu).

42
Festival of the
Dragon-boat[1] on the
Fifth Day of the
Fifth Moon

THE destinies of the empire are said to be under the tutelage of four supernatural animals — the stag, tortoise, phœnix, and dragon. The first presides over literature, and is visible at the birth of sages; the second over virtue, and appears at periods of widespread morality, or perhaps on occasions of general peace; the third controls knowledge of the future; and the dragon represents authority. This last extraordinary monster is the national ensign of China; it is painted on their standards, attached to precepts, edicts, documents, books, and all imperial instruments or insignia. Besides his possession of authority, the dragon influences the seasons, and exerts a decided mastery over the heavenly bodies. Eclipses have always hitherto yielded to his ravenous inclinations, which leads him occasionally to swallow the sun and moon, leaving the empire in total darkness. To appease his wrath, to divert his attention from these serious pursuits, the festival of the Dragon Boat is instituted, and held on the fifth day of the fifth moon, which generally falls in June.

A boat of trifling width, but long enough to accommodate from forty to sixty paddles, is built for the occasion, having a figure-head representing the Chinese imperial emblem. As it cuts through the water with a rapidity which so great a thrust necessarily compels, the shouts of spectators, sounds of wind-instruments, and rolling of drums, lend increased vigour to the boatmen, whose sacred vessel not unfrequently comes into collision with lesser bodies, over which it passes almost imperceptibly, to all but the sufferers. A monster drum, with a well-stretched ox-hide for its head, placed amidships, is beaten heroically by three stout players; these strike simultaneously; whilst a professional clown, at their side, continues, with increasing activity, to make grimaces, rise on his toes, sink on his haunches, sneer, snarl, look up towards the sky, and wind his arms about, to the cadences of the great drum. On the little deck at the boat's head, two men are stationed, armed with long sharp-pointed halberts; and their particular duty is to shout, and brandish their weapons in the most menacing manner. The Dragon, although fervently adored as being capable of good, is also servilely feared as the author of evil, and it is for this purpose that he is believed to conceal himself at certain periods in the little creeks, and under the shelving banks of the river. The Chinese sailor lives in constant fear of being overturned by the malice of the Dragon who darts out suddenly from his ambush upon the unsuspecting victim. The inconsistency of superstition is strongly marked in this national festival; for, the very deity to whom they ascribe the possession of authority at all other times, in the month of June they undertake to put down, or frighten away.

---

[1] *This view was taken opposite the European factories at Canton.*

43
Sacrifice of the Ching-tswe-tsee, or Harvest-moon

CHINESE religious observances are divided into three classes — great (ta,) medium (choong,) and lesser (seaou.) Amongst the second kind are those made upon the gathering in of harvest, which are accompanied by the genial quality of gratitude.

When the day of the full harvest-moon arrives, Chinamen, wherever they may be, or however engaged, with a sort of Mussulman scrupulosity, make their offerings to the gods of grain and of land. In every city, usually where the highways meet, this offering to the Chinese god of grain is made. Generally a stone is set up for a harvest-god, before which incense is burned; and logs of wood, hewn into imperfect resemblances of the "human form divine," are placed around, to represent rustic deities, local genii, tutelar gods of agriculture, horticulture, and rural occupations; these effigies being, in some instances, brazenly passed off upon spectators as appropriate representations of the sun, moon, clouds, winds, rain, and thunder.

Even those who happen to be at sea, or navigating the great rivers of the empire, when the day of the full harvest-moon arrives, are under an obligation to sacrifice to the gods or goddesses of plenty, whom they especially adore.

When the harvest-moon is at the full, the China-man holds his agricultural festival, unimpeded in his religious duties by the claims of those that are temporal; the labours of the barn, performed by the flail — the operation of winnowing, in which a bamboo sieve and spacious cotton sheet are the only implements — and the preparation of the fields for another crop of rice, all "go bravely on," while the family, in the attitude of prayer and thankfulness, are engaged before the altar of their rural gods. In the vicinity of the farm-buildings, but always in an open position, a portico is constructed, in a style of especial neatness, for the reception of the image selected by the head of the family. A table in front of the niche in which the crude figure is set up, serves as an altar on which flowers, and pastiles, and tapers, are ranged, with cups of rice or tea. Here, the mother of the family presents herself, holding in her apron such produce and grain as she deems most suitable for a first-fruits offering. Behind and beside her on a mat spread out before the rustic temple, her husband and children attend, and second her intreaties that the offering may be accepted, by prostrations and silent prayers.

The accompanying view, which represents a rice-farm a few li from Yang-tcheou, is remarkably characteristic, conveying a most full representation of the national habits and local scenery. A town of the third class, with its pagoda towering over it, fills the remote distance; the rice-grounds, in preparation for a second crop, occupy the middle; while the harvest sacrifice, and reduction of the crop just saved to a marketable state, take up the whole foreground of this epitome of utilitarianism.

In this little scene, that cannot be viewed without an affecting interest — without increasing, or rather creating, a respect for the charactor of the rural population of this vast empire, the uses of the national tree, the bamboo, are more than ordinarily conspicuous. The shed, and gates, and fence of the threshing-stall are of split stems; the sieve used by the winnower, the large mat on which the family are kneeling before the altar, the hat worn by the patriarch, the table under the portico, and the entire of the temple itself, are composed of the stems, or the canes, or the fibres of this invaluable plant.

VI
CHINESE AMUSEMENTS

IN one respect at least the Chinese are found to be no different from the rest of humanity — that is, in their love for various forms of amusement and entertainment. In traditional China there was to be found the whole gamut of pastimes and entertainments as is to be encountered elsewhere — the theatre, music, acrobatics and juggling, cards, chess and even punch and judy shows. Games in the sense of sports did not truly exist, although the shuttlecock was kicked about — it was for the British to educate the world in this; but the Chinese shared the British addiction for games of chance, except on an even more general scale. However, as one would suppose, the Chinese version of all these things was markedly different. The conventions of stage and opera were quite different, the structure of Chinese music was quite different, so much so that Westerners could usually only endure it as a hardship, and Chinese cards were different, and Chinese chess was different. Nevertheless, having taken all these deviations from the Western norm into account, the fact remains — and was well in evidence in the nineteenth century — that the Chinese valued being amused and entertained as much as Queen Victoria or anyone else.

44
Ladies of a Mandarin's Family at Cards

THE variety of games known in China is endless; and many of them require considerable skill. As for card games, in shape, the cards are longer and narrower than those in use amongst Europeans, and a pack includes a much larger number. When cards have lost their power of pleasing, the time is beguiled by the introduction of tobacco. Females, from the tender age of eight years, are initiated in this disgusting habit; and a little silken reticule is generally attached to every lady's dress, to hold a pipe and a supply of tobacco. But these, and even less graceful employments, are pardonable, when the monotonous nature of their life of seclusion is remembered. Although less suspected, less enslaved, less degraded than Turkish females, yet the formality to which Chinese ladies are doomed is eminently tedious. Children, chief comfort of a mother's retired and useful life, are in China placed under laws that outrage the best feelings of human nature. Female infants may be destroyed at the pleasure of the father — over children of the other sex, the law gives the parent absolute power; hence, at the age of ten years, the boy is removed finally from the mother's surveillance, nor is he permitted after to visit the pavilion in which he was born — the scene in which his helplessness first found that care which a mother only knows how to bestow. Cut off, by a hateful code of regulations, from the opportunity of fulfilling her legitimate trust, the Chinese wife and mother is necessitated to have recourse to those means of filling up the great void in life which these privations have created. Painting, embroidery, the care of an aviary, the recreations of the garden and the pleasure grounds, occasional appeals to the little image that presides over the domestic altar,[1] fond attentions to her children while they are permitted to remain with her, the game of chess when the number of fair captives is limited to two, but, when increased beyond that amount, the more popular amusement of cards, are called to the relief of those pangs which disappointments produce — those sorrows by which separation from the world is so often accompanied.

---

[1] *Note the family altar in the background of this picture.*

This picture is another Allom adaptation, taken from Alexander's River Scene, Tientsin, *drawn during the course of the Macartney embassy of 1793.*

THE conflux of the rivers Pei-ho and Eu-ho, the former opening a communication with the capital, eighty miles distant, and with the sea, fifty miles; the latter, by means of the imperial canal, with all the southern provinces, conferred an early commercial importance upon Tien-sin.[1]

In the most busy and populous commercial towns, where labour appears only to cease when the labourer is at the end of his physical powers, the greatest variety of public shows and entertainments, the largest number of coffee-houses, restaurateurs, assembly-rooms, and theatres, are always found; a sufficient evidence that in such localities they receive the largest share of patronage. This remark applies with more than common appropriateness to Tien-sin, which has long been celebrated as the chief place of trade in the province,[2] as well as for its everlasting scenes of recreation and gaiety.

Twice have our embassies passed and repassed this great emporium.[3]

It was on the first of these occasions, while the state-barges lay moored before the viceroy's palace, that a temporary theatre was erected on the quay, with a gaily dressed orchestra behind it, in which a dramatic entertainment, after the national manner, was represented, for the gratification of the embassy. The exterior of the building was decorated

45
Theatre at Tien Sin

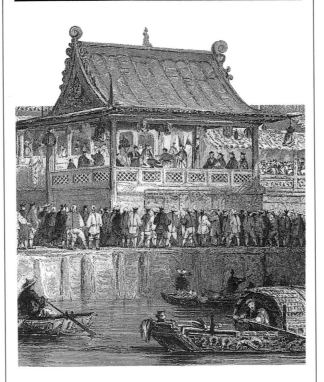

with a variety of brilliant and lively colours, by the proper distribution, as well as contrast of which, the Chinese are able to produce the most pleasing effects. The front was left completely open towards the river, and the interior adorned with the same elegance and success. The performance was continued without interruption during a whole day, pantomime and historic dramas taking alternate possession of the boards. Strict attention was paid to costume, the actors being uniformly clothed in the ancient dresses of the age in which the personages represented were supposed to have lived. A kind of recitative supplied the place of dialogue, accompanied by a variety of musical instruments, in which the gong, kettle-drum, and trumpet were conspicuous, each pause being filled up by a loud crash, such as our "brass bands" sometimes introduce. Every actor announced on his first entrance the part he was about to perform, — where the scene was laid, and other explanatory details; but this is only observed when the audience are foreigners, or not well acquainted with the language of China.

---

[1] *Tientsin became a well-known name in the West after the Treaty of 1858 signed there to conclude the Second Opium War. The Treaty was later expanded and confirmed by the Convention of Peking (1861).*

[2] *The former province of Chihli (now broken up into smaller divisions).*

[3] *Referring to the embassies of Lords Macartney (1793) and Amherst (1816).*

46
Kite-flying at Hae-kwan

AMONG all the sports and festivals of the Chinese, cricket and quail-fighting, shuttlecock-playing, the game of mora,[1] or odd and even, prevail in every province of the empire: and to these very ancient indulgences, is to be added the favourite amusement of kite-flying. Fond of tricks, conjuring, display of muscular flexibility on all occasions, the kite-flyer endeavours to infuse some share of these qualities into his favourite employment. Bamboo-cane is peculiarly suitable, from its flexibility, as the leader and cross-piece of a kite; and there is a species of paper, made from the floss or refuse of silk, that is both tough and light, which is particularly serviceable in covering a skeleton made of cane and cord. Dexterous in every manipulatory art, the Chinaman has of course attained to excellence in the construction of kites, and he proceeds to decorate them with the most fanciful ornaments, as well as to shape them into forms borrowed from those of the animal kingdom. Eagles, owls, and the whole feathered tribe, furnish originals for imitation in the structure of a kite; and when raised on high with outspread wings, and painted feathers, and eyes of transparent glass, they represent their prototype with the utmost fidelity. It is an established custom to devote the ninth day of the ninth moon, as the special festival of this amusement; and on this joyous occasion children and aged men unite in the exhilarating pleasures of a whole holiday's kite-flying, on the most elevated place in the suburbs of each town. The panoramic view from "the hill of beauty," that hangs over the rich valley of Hae-kwan, cannot fail to increase the pleasurable feelings that attend the sport; and the townspeople themselves feel fully alive to the charms of the spot, by the fulness of their attendance at these ancient festivities. When the appetite for mirth and fun, as well as the hours of the day itself, are nearly exhausted, the performers endeavour to bring their kites into collision, or rather try to break each other's strings by crossing. Should they not succeed in this attempt, they give the sportive effigies to the wind, to be borne whither their destinies may lead them. One of the chief improvements in this manufacture, which the Chinese arrogate to themselves, is the introduction of numerous cords strained across apertures in the paper. The resistance of the air acting on these little bars, produces a continued humming noise; and when many kites are flown in company the combined tones are both loud and agreeable.

---

[1]*For the meaning and description of this game, see p. 97.*

[1]For the meaning and description of this game, see p. 97.

47
Playing at Shuttlecock with the Feet

NEAR to the confluence of the Tchang-ho with the Cha-ho, river of flood-gates, or imperial canal, is a splendid octagonal pagoda: it consists of nine stories, adorned with projecting eves, and it tapers with a remarkably gradual and graceful convergence. From its base to the edge of the waters, the grounds slope gently, and this pleasant area being reserved for the recreation of the citizens of Lin-tsing-choo, generally presents a scene of mirth, although not always of morality. Here jugglers display their unrivaled dexterity in the arts of deception; tumblers, vaulters, and clowns exhibit feats in which the strength and suppleness of the human body are conspicuously shown, and old pulcinello,[1] long-admired of civilized Europeans, asserts his claims to a pre-eminence. However, the kingdom of fun is yet extended further by dishonest and vicious devotees of chance. Building, with a certainty but too secure, upon the evil propensities of our nature, quail[2] and cricket fighters, mora[3] players, and gamblers of every description known in this wide empire, here congregate, to exercise their demoralizing callings, and accelerate the ruin of thousands who become the easy dupes of their villany.

Around the groups engaged with absorbing earnestness in games of chance, the more cautious, but not less interested, are seated, relieving their anxiety upon the pending bet, by the pleasures of the chibouque.[4] There are, however, other, and these rather numerous groups, more innocently occupied with either feats of activity or sports, which, though probably little suited to their advanced years, are exercises of virtue in comparison with the occupations in which their fellows are engaged on the greensward all around them. Kite-flying, for example, constitutes a favourite amusement, and few nations have ever succeeded, possibly none have ever aspired, to elevate these simple articles to such a height as the Chinese.

Celestial taste is not confined, however, to this innocent amusement; the sport of shuttlecock, certainly a healthy recreation, is pursued with a degree of enthusiasm which it is seldom known to excite in the western world. There it is strictly limited to the youth of both sexes, and in some resigned to the gentler exclusively; but, in China, the most muscular men amongst the labouring classes seem to feel inexpressible delight in the sensation it produces. No battle-doors[5] are employed, nor are the hands generally of any service in the game, save to balance the player's body during its rapid movements: the shuttlecock is struck with the soles of the feet, sometimes unprotected by any covering; at others, however, wooden shoes are permitted, and the noise which these clumsy togs contribute, is considered to add to the general amusement. Five, frequently six persons, form themselves into a circle, for the purpose of playing at this active game; and whether shoes be permitted, or hands occasionally allowed, to aid the feet in preventing the shuttlecock from coming to the ground, the least successful players fall out of the ring in turn, until the number is gradually reduced to one; this one is, of course, declared to be the winner of the stakes, or the pool, or the object played for, whatever it may happen to have been.

---

[1] *Pulcinello, Punch of the Punch and Judy show, a word of Italian origin.*

[2] *See p. 97.*

[3] *Refer to p. 97.*

[4] *A long Turkish tobacco pipe, as seen being used by the spectator leaning against the temple wall on the far left of this picture.*

[5] *Battledore, or 'bat', the striker used to hit shuttlecocks with in the West.*

48
Raree-show[1] at Lin-sin-choo

THE IMPERIAL CANAL commences, correctly speaking, at the city of Lin-sin-choo, in the province of Shan-tung. The vicinity of Lin-sin-choo has long been the rendesvouz of carriers, who here transfer their burdens from one description of junk to another, — exchange commodities, engage and dismiss trackers, or transact other matters, necessarily connected with an *entrepôt* so centrally situated for inland trade.

The concourse of merchants, dealers, travellers, bargemen, in addition to the civic functionaries, and the number of retainers neccessary to preserve order amongst a population that is constantly *in transitu*, present peculiar attractions to strolling players, jugglers, and charlatans of all descriptions; and the streets of Lin-sin-choo are continually animated by the performances of these ministers of mirth.

It is from this ancient empire that the very amusements of the humbler classes, both on the European continent and in Great Britain, have obviously been derived. The *Ombres Chinoises* indicates their country sufficiently by their name; and in the puppet figures of the Chinese raree-showmen are recognized the originals of the Fantoccini of Italy, and the Punch and Judy of more western countries.

The Chinese Punch is performed by a person mounted on a stool, and concealed, *as far as the ankle*, with blue drapery. On his head rests a box or stage, such as Punchinello[2] is generally performed in, and the figures are put in motion by the insertion of the manager's fingers into their arms. This is the principle, the practice being somewhat altered, on which the celebrated Punch and Judy show is now conducted.

Both in England and in China, music forms a necessary part of the entertainment: Mr. Allom's[3]

musician at Lin-sin-choo seems to be very fully occupied, and resolutely bent upon diverting the attention of the spectators from those movements of the mechanism, or from that sleight-of-hand which might detract from the general effect of the exhibition. To his left foot a cymbal is attached, which he strikes against its fellow fixed securely on the ground, with his right foot he plays upon a drum or tambour, while both hands are employed in the management of a *hwang-teih*, or flute, occasionally exchanged for the *heang-teih*, or clarionet, that is suspended at his side. This immense instrument is simply a bamboo cane, having a mouth-hole at some distance from the end, a second aperture, covered with the inner rind or film of a species of reed, two inches lower down, besides ten ventiges, six of which are effective and equidistant. The tone of the bamboo flute is both sweet and powerful, and the harmony of the musician's little band, in general, agreeable.

Although the spectators and auditors at the raree-show in Lin-sin-choo belong to the industrious and humbler classes, puppet-shows, the probable original of the regular drama, are here not the peculiar entertainment of these classes; on the contrary, they are patronized by the imperial household, and are included in the court amusements.

---

[1] *'Show carried about in a box, peep-show'* (rare show *as pronounced by Italian showmen), according to the* Oxford English Dictionary.

[2] *Refer to note 1 on p. 93.*

[3] *More correctly, 'Mr Alexander's musician' because this is an Allom adaptation from the former's plate in* Picturesque Representations.

49
Canton Bargemen, Fighting Quails

GAMING amongst the Chinese is analogous to the tricks and swindling practised at our country fairs, and on every race-course, with this difference only, that cards are there in more general demand. The athletic bargemen on the Pearl river, devote every hour, that can be stolen from work, to the recreation of gambling; and, the weary trader buries all his sorrows in the excitement which this activity awakes. Children partake of this national pastime in some degree, or rather the vicious habits of society create an appetite in the youthful mind. A fruit-vender disposes of his goods by a sort of lottery, or game of hazard; supplied with a box and dice, he presents them to his customer, who stakes the price against the selected fruits. The first throw is the buyer's privilege, and the winner, of course, takes up both fruit and money. Raffling is also a favourite mode of barter; provisions of every description are disposed of in this way, and so completely does vice obtain mastery, that wives, or children, are sometimes the last stake played for between these habitual gamblers.

Dominoes, dice, and cards constitute the chief instruments of this trade; and chess is also generally known. Their cards are seldom more than three inches in length by one in breadth, and marked with red and black colours as our own. The suspense, and the consumption of time, inseparable from a long-contested game of chess, in which, after all, the victory is a triumph of memory rather than discernment, have caused it to be less popular than most others; but, such are the industry and perseverance of the Chinese, that when they do prefer it, they are admirable players.

"Hunt-the-slipper," a game familiar in England is probably a mere version of the Chinese "Hand-the-flower." While the bouquet rapidly passes from hand to hand, a continued roll is kept up on a drum in an adjoining room; whoever happens to have the bouquet at the moment when the roll ceases, drinks an extra cup of wine, or pays for a cup "all round." But of all the games in use amongst the humbler classes in China, the *Tsoi-moi* is the most popular: "Two persons, sitting directly opposite to each other, raise their hands at the same moment, when each calls out the number he guesses to be the sum of the fingers expanded by himself and his adversary. The closed hand or fist is none — the thumb, one — the thumb and forefinger, two — and so on; the chances lying between 0 and 5, as each must know the number held out by himself."[1]

There are other sports and gambling practices, which are to be added to those already noticed; they include cock-fighting, a favourite amusement of the Mandarins, which was probably imported from the country of the Malays; quail and cricket fighting, — all equally cruel and unmanly. Training is a profession which gives occupation to many, and the interest taken in these sports is universal. The birds are furnished with steel spurs, as our game-cocks in the pit, and the contest, therefore, seldom fails to prove fatal to one or both. The victor is put up for sale, or raffle, and the eagerness to become his master is demonstrated by the enormous sums staked, or paid down, for him.[2]

---

[1] *The game is known as* mora *in the West; the origin of* mora *is Italian, and the game was most popular in that country.*

[2] *Quail fighting was just another variant of the cock-fighting just described.*

50
Jugglers Exhibiting in the Court of a Mandarin's House

WHEN the banquet is finally ended in a great man's palace, the guests are conducted to an open court, surrounded by pavilions, and decorated with china vases, aromatic plants, and gorgeous lanterns. Here a company of fortune-tellers, with their sticks of fate — conjurors with cards and dice, and well skilled in sleight-of-hand — tumblers, capable of performing evolutions, displaying agility, muscular strength, and suppleness, not equalled beyond the limits of the olden world, is assembled. The display of keeping four, and even five balls, cups, or knives, in constant gyration, has been made by Chinese and Hindoos in England; but not the performance of the same feat with two balls and three knives together. This difficult exploit was very popular in ancient Rome, where the knife-catchers were called *ventilatores*, and the ball-throwers, *pilarii*. The Chinese, however, perform a greater number and much more artful tricks than the Hindoos. It is not uncommon to see a performer balance on his forehead a little building, consisting of a number of pieces of wood, which would all fall apart, if the balance were not the most exact; and, during this feat, the actor keeps a number of rings in motion with this toes, in a manner that seems to require the greatest attention. Stringing pearls with the tongue — swallowing a sword-blade — carrying about the person, and producing them unexpectedly, large china bowls, full of water to the brim, and flower-

pots with plants of two feet in height standing in them — changing the colour of powders, almost under the watchful gaze of the spectator — drawing many different kinds of wine from the same column in the dining-parlour, by piercing it with a gimlet[1] — swallowing and disgorging miles' length of paper shreds, and tossing a brass ring, which the company are at liberty to examine minutely, into the air, where it separates into two, then four, then six rings, of equal size with the original, and, as they fall into the hand, forming them into various mathematical combinations, are amongst the variety of illusions practised by Chinese conjurors.

---

[1] *A small boring instrument.*

VII
CHINESE PUNISHMENTS

There is not too much to be said about traditional Chinese punishments except that — outlandish though they may have appeared to Victorian eyes — they were in general applied with moderation, and, in any case, were no more severe (often far less) than the punishments which were imposed for similar offences in most Western states at this period. In theory Chinese punishments for specific crimes could be indeed harsh and severe; in practice they were in general imposed with leniency and commonsense.

51
Punishment of the Pan-tze, or Bastinado

THE PAN-TZE, or Bastinado,[1] is the punishment most frequently inflicted in every part of China, and for almost every species of offence, the number of blows being regulated by the magnitude of the guilt. The culprit is usually brought to some public place outside the city walls, and, in presence of a mandarin and guard of soldiers, beaten by slaves kept for the purpose. If the crime be serious, and a proportionate punishment to be inflicted, the criminal is held down by one or more slaves, while the chief actor furnished with a half-bamboo, six feet in length and about two inches broad, strikes him on the back part of the thighs. Upon the termination of this degrading ceremony, the offender, impressed with the habitual feeling that he has been flogged like a schoolboy for his future benefit, falls prostrate before the attending mandarin, and returns thanks for his parental vigilance and concern.

The Pan-tze is rendered almost fashionable by the example of the court, and the universality of its application. "Each officer of state, from the ninth degree upwards to the fourth, can at any time administer a gentle correction to his inferior; and the emperor orders the bamboo to his ministers, and to the other four classes, whenever he may think it necessary for the good of their morals." The emperor Kien-Long[2] ordered two of his sons to be bambooed long after had reached to the age of maturity, and one of these princes afterwards succeeded him on the throne.

It is some satisfaction to the poor, that the rich are also included under the same criminal code; but, as the administration of the Pan-tze is often entrusted to men of cruel dispositions, the highest injustice constantly disfigures the whole executive system. A Chinaman generally submits with patience to his fate, but a Tartar never gives thanks to the mandarin, recollecting that his nation subdued the Chinese, and concluding therefore that they have no right to flog him. The paternal origin and nature of the bastinado are still more distinctly shown during the ceremony, the sufferer having the privilege of exemption from every fifth blow, if he demands it as the emperor's *coup-de-grace;* but what he gains by diminished numbers, he most probably loses by increased severity.

---

[1] *The dictionary definition of* bastinado — *a Spanish word — is punishment by caning the soles of the feet, so that it does not represent an accurate translation of the Chinese practice of* pan-tze.

[2] *The Ch'ien-lung Emperor, (1735–96), the sixth ruler of the Ch'ing dynasty.*

52
Punishment of the Tcha, or Cangue, Ting-hai

As acknowledged, this picture is based on a drawing by Warner Varnham, an English tea-inspector at Canton who was also a pupil of the painter, George Chinnery, at Macao.

FOR offences of a somewhat grave description, the Tcha, or Cangue, is one of the most frequent and distressing. Its severity, however, lays more in mental agony than bodily suffering, and in this property consists its virtue. The instrument itself is a heavy wooden frame-work, formed of two sections fastened at one end by a hinge, and at the other by a lock or screw. The neck of the culprit passes through a hole in the centre, and his hands through smaller apertures on each side. Sometimes he is indulged with the freedom of one hand, which he employs in relieving the weight of the cangue from his bruised shoulders.

Over the screw which secures the sections enclosing the offender's neck, a paper is generally pasted, to which is affixed the seal or chop of the committing mandarin; and over another part of the log, a placard setting forth the crime which has merited this degradation.

The weight of these moveable pillories is from sixty to two hundred pounds avoirdupois, and the time of endurance is proportioned, according to the judgment of the magistrate, to the magnitude of the offence. A criminal has been known to endure a heavy cangue for half a year, passing his nights in the dungeons of Ting-hai, and, when day appeared, led by a chain to the most frequented of the city-gates. The keeper, armed with a thick bamboo, or large thong-whip, conducts him to some position where he may recline against a wall, and ease his shoulders of their ponderous load. If both the culprit's hands be confined, he cannot raise food or drink to his mouth, in which case the attendant feeds him with the miserable jail-allowance; or some compassionate occupants of the adjoining houses, near to which he happens to be placed for the day, supply him with refreshments. One of the aggravations of this collar of infamy is the ridicule to which the wearer is exposed from all the idle urchins that crowd the streets, at his inability to feed himself, and at the total dependence of one, who was once as powerful as profligate, upon the compassion and benevolence of those whom possibly he may fomerly have wronged.

But the offended majesty of Chinese law does not become appeased on all occasions by the imposition of the cangue; sometimes the mandarins think proper to inflict a number of blows with the bamboo on the liberated wearer; sometimes banishment from the district is added; and, should the offence be deemed unpardonable, though still not deserving of capital punishment, perpetual exile from the empire is decreed.

VIII
CHINA
AT WAR

In Chinese eyes the First Opium War was about opium, and sprang from the attempt to suppress that prohibited trade which, aided and abetted by foreign merchants (especially the British), was expanding uncontrollably. This traffic was not only injurious in human terms; it was also bad for the economy. To add insult to injury, the foreign traders (especially the British) failed to respect Chinese conventions and aspired to place the actions of their countrymen on Chinese soil beyond the reach of Chinese justice. The main issue for the British was conditions of trade. This trade was confined to one port and conducted through a monopoly of Chinese merchants (the Co-hong). Tariffs were arbitrary, Chinese norms of justice unacceptable, and there was no means of appeal to the lords of the land because all diplomatic relations had to be channelled through the Co-hong. In short, the Chinese on the one hand wanted to dispose of the opium problem once and for all and to defend their sovereign rights; the British, on the other, wanted to alter the terms of trade in their favour and to gain unfettered access to the vast Chinese market.

Whether opium was at the root of the conflict or not, it certainly was the immediate cause. To suppress the trade completely, a special Imperial Commissioner was appointed. On his arrival at Canton in early 1839, Chinese dealers in opium were put in chains, their stocks confiscated, and the foreign traders were told that they could remain only against a pledge to have nothing more to do with opium, and to hand over all the opium in their possession. The opium was eventually surrendered and destroyed, but the refusal of the British to sign the pledge resulted in deadlock. The British then sought backing from home. A bellicose Palmerston at the British Foreign Office ensured that the backing was not long in coming. Within six months a powerful British naval squadron dropped anchor in Chinese waters, bent on action. In the meantime hostilities had already broken out locally.

During the three years of war the actual fighting was limited and spasmodic, and the outcome never in doubt. The British navy ruled the waves. The Chinese were quickly bottled up in their ports while the naval force moved purposefully north until it become a direct threat to the imperial capital. Now acting with a realism hitherto absent in their dealings with the foreigner, the imperial authorities speedily accepted the peace terms given to them. By the Treaty of Nanking (1842) the British succeeded (or appeared to have succeeded) in achieving their main purposes. The Co-hong was abolished; five ports were opened to British trade; Hong Kong was ceded as a British base; equality of diplomatic status was recognized; a fixed tariff system was promised; and adequate compensation for the expenses of the war was given.

For the British the war was a walkover. Although their 60 ships and 10,000 soldiers could not compete in numbers with the 430 millions of the Chinese Empire, the Manchu weapons that had conquered China itself two hundred years before were no match for the ordnance of Queen Victoria's navy. In the seventeen or so sporadic engagements that took place, the tale was always the same. Gallant resistance was reduced within minutes by a naval broadside, with large casualties on the one side and barely a scratch on the other. The British losses from enemy action in the entire war never amounted to more than what one could expect in a bad Victorian train crash. For the Chinese the war was an unmitigated disaster in terms of the toll on human life, the destruction of property and the harm to the national interest. After 1842 China lay at the mercy of the West, and it was to take another hundred years of reverse and humiliation before the country recovered its sovereignty and self-respect.

53
Joss-house,[1] Chapoo, Death of Col. Tomlinson

THE fall of Chapoo and death of Colonel Tomlinson have been described:[2] the accompanying view, taken almost immediately after the bloody conflict which it so vividly portrays, places before the reader the local features of the scene at which it occurred.

In other countries, as well as in China, temples of religious worship have been converted into places of temporary defence, in time of war, and garrisoned by gallant companies that have done honour to their country. The positions of churches, having a tower well suited for a military post, from which musketry can act, with dreadful effect, upon an assailing party, render their occupancy always a point of importance. And it may accordingly be observed, that the most fatal encounters, in every aggressive war, have arisen from a struggle for their possession. The death of Colonel Tomlinson was attended with circumstances of greater gallantry than any other event in the Chinese war; and the obstinate defence of the Joss-house at Chapoo may be cited by the Tartars, as an evidence of their personal bravery.

---

[1] *A temple, joss being a term for a Chinese idol.*
[2] *See p. 117.*

54
The Tai-wang-kow, or Yellow Pagoda Fort,[1] Canton River

AN islet that seems to float in the channel, called by Europeans the Macao Passage, serves as the foundation for the fortified pagoda of the Tai-wang-kow. A tower of four stories is enclosed by a strongly built curtain of granite stone, pierced with loop-holes, and finished with battlements. The prime purpose of the Pagoda is not easily explicable on rational principles; but, in connection with the Chinese system of military discipline, and their art of war, admits of explanation. From the eleva-tion of its turreted stories, watchmen can discern the approaching enemy, and give the word of command to the gunners within the ramparts. This plan, however, is subject to one inconvenience, namely, discovery of the fort itself by the foe, and, therefore, exposure of the Pagoda itself to the fire of an enemy's ship, which might throw down the whole building upon the gunners at its foot. In this case, the gingalls,[2] matchlocks,[3] and men of all arms, would in all probability be buried in the ruins. The area of the island, about an English acre, is dedicated to military works, with the exception of the space occupied by some lofty trees of the banyan species, whose shelter proves particularly grateful to the soldier sinking under the weight of his armour, and who would otherwise often be ex-hausted by the scorching rays of a tropical sun. The practice of enclosing a fortress by trees is not confined to Tai-wang-kow, it prevails everywhere in Chinese defensive posts, engineers being of opinion, that the shade of a banyan tree will protect the soldier not only from the burning rays of the sun, but also from the red artillery of an enemy. And it was this principle of self-sufficiency or self-deception, so prevalent in this vast empire, that induced the erection of a pagoda in the middle of a battery, which, to be useful, should be concealed, — the author of the design imagining that its haughty height would warn the enemy against too near an approach.

Upon the first appearance of a rupture with China, this picturesque defence was occupied by a detachment of the royal marines, who kept entire possession of it until the resumption of hostilities on the 23d of June, 1841.[4] Although within reach of assistance from Canton, from which it is only two miles distant, no resistance was offered to our occu-pation; yet our officers assert, that had they been attacked in turn, they could have repulsed the best efforts of the enemy to dislodge them. As a toll-house or watch-tower, the Tai-wang is valuable, and in other hands, by its means, the approach of an enemy to Canton might be successfully impeded. When our troops surprised it, they found a connection formed with both banks of the river by rafts that completely obstructed the river channels. Each flotilla, or rather section of the pontoon, consisted of ten layers of timber, ten feet square, stongly bound together with iron bolts, and anchored securely at each corner. There was little ingenuity in the design, and when our troops entered the fort, and occupied it, the control of the clumsy obstacle passed into their hands, to the disadvantage of its builders.

---

[1] *Or Ta-huang-chiao, after the Chinese name for the waterway on which it stood. It is probably the 'Macao Fort' of the British records, which was occupied on 13 March 1841 after the breakdown of the agreement signed at Chuenpi the previous January.*

[2] *Gingal or jingal: a kind of gun, from 6 to 14 feet in length, carried on the shoulders of two men and fired by a third, used on land and sea; they are supposed to have been the weapon which gave the Manchus the upper hand in the conquest of China.*

[3] *Old-fashioned gun with a receptacle or lock for powder, to be lighted with a match.*

[4] *This is inaccurate: the British, having invested Canton in May 1841, withdrew, on receiving payment of a ransom to spare the city, at the beginning of June. The British reoccupied the fort and re-sumed the blockade of Canton in August, while the main fleet sailed north to threaten Peking.*

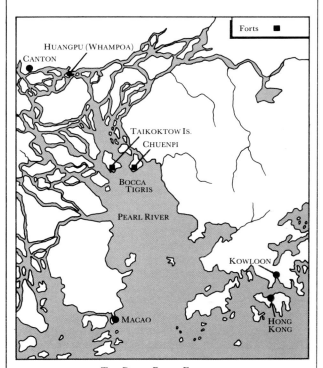

THE PEARL RIVER ESTUARY

55
Attack and Capture of Chuenpee[1] (7 January 1841)

THE principal entrance of the Pearl river is between Chuenpee and Tycocktow forts, the outer defences of that great emporium, the city of Canton. To the west is an extensive delta, intersected by numerous branches; all, however, too shallow for any other than flat-bottomed craft: but with these a considerable trade is carried on between Canton and Macao. During the opium war, the English commanders, through the effrontery and arrogance of Commissioner Lin,[2] were compelled to attack and capture Chuenpee. The accompanying plate represents that achievement.

[1] Or Chuenpi, a small settlement where the Shatok fort, one of the key emplacements (together with the fort on the island of Taikoktow opposite) guarding the entrance to the Pearl River leading up to Canton, was situated. Apart from the action illustrated here, Chuenpi was also the scene of an earlier clash (3 November 1839) which marked the undeclared start of the Opium War. It was also the place which gave its name to the abortive Convention of Chuenpi signed two weeks after the attack shown here.

[2] Lin Tse-hsu (Lin Zexu) was the Imperial Commissioner appointed by the Peking Court to suppress the opium trade in early 1839. His 'effrontery and arrogance' consisted of his attempts to carry out his commission. However the British attack on the Shatok and Taikoktow forts on 7 January 1841 was not precipitated by Lin who was already in disgrace for his failure to deal effectively with the British. It was the result of the refusal of his successor, Ki-shen (Qishan), to accept the British demand for the cession of Hong Kong, despite his generally conciliatory policy, for he knew that Peking would never agree. The attack on the forts produced the Convention of Chuenpi signed by the British and Ki-shen but immediately disavowed by Peking. As a result Ki-shen also fell into disgrace, and returned to Peking a prisoner in irons.

56
Entrance to the Chin-chew River, Fokien

IN its progress northward, after Amoy had been captured, the British fleet entered the estuary of the Chin-chew river, on the south bank of which, but some miles inland, the city of Tscuen-tcheou-foo[1] is situated. As this port was the very focus of the contraband traffic in opium, some rude preparations had been made to resist the approach of a hostile expedition. Description of those operations is superseded by the intelligible, and very clever drawings of the scene, which the portfolio of Captain Stoddart, a member of the expedition, placed under Mr. Allom's control. The Chinese junks kept at a respectful distance, from the boats of the detachment that was ordered to effect a landing at the foot of a bluff on the north side of the river, and, as to the brave Tartars, who were placed there to serve the guns on shore, after a few discharges only, they fled in the wildest dismay, abandoning their copper cannon and all their ammunition to the enemy. The material of which they were made, rendered the captured cannon something more than trophies of glory: the value of those taken at Chin-hae alone, exceeded £10,000 sterling; and the spoils of Woosung were still more important.

The commercial city, to which the Chin-chew river is the highway, holds a distinguished place amongst those of the first class:[2] inferior to few in geographical position, and in healthful trade, it is eminently adorned with triumphal arches, temples, and other public edifices, its streets being remarkable for their extent and width. Seven cities of the third of the third rank are placed under the protection of this ancient and populous fou. It is in the immediate vicinity of Tsuen-tcheou, that the extraordinary bridge[3] is to be seen, which has been described in the following terms:– "It is built entirely of a blackish stone, and has no arches, but upwards of three hundred large stone pillars, which terminate on each side in an acute angle, to break the violence of the current with great facility. Five stones of equal size, laid transversely from one pillar to another, form the breadth of the bridge, each of which, according to the measurement made in walking, was eighteen of ordinary steps in length; there are one thousand of them, all of the same size and figure: a wonderful work, when one considers the great number of these heavy stones, and the manner in which they are supported between the pillars. On each side there are buttresses or props, constructed of the same kind of stone, on the tops of which are placed lions on pedestals, and other ornaments of a similar description." Many lives having been lost while ferry-boats were the only means of crossing these troubled waters, a certain humane governor of the city constructed this splendid monument to his fame, at his sole expense. That expense, if reliance may be placed on the accounts of the learned Du Halde,[4] amounted to half a million sterling.

---

[1] *Changchow, which is possibly the site of the once fabulous city of Zayton (known to Arab sailors and conducting a prodigious trade with Indian ports in the seventh and eighth centuries AD), the source of the word 'satin' and an early centre of the tea trade.*

[2] *For the classification of Chinese cities, see p. 12.*

[3] *This 1100 foot-long bridge, constructed of huge slabs of granite weighing an average of 200 tons apiece, is still in existence.*

[4] *Du Halde was a member of the Jesuit mission at Peking during the days of its favour in the late seventeenth century.*

57
Capture of Ting-hai, Chusan[1]

TWICE, during the protracted hostilities between Great Britain and China, has this rich and beautiful position fallen before the courage and military skill of the former; and the morning of the 5th of July, 1840, was the day fated for Her Majesty's flag to wave over the most beautiful island appertaining to the Celestial empire, the first European banner that has floated over the flowery land. A few words, however, will be sufficient to describe this easy conquest. At half-past two o'clock the Wellesley fired the first gun, which was answered by a whole line of war junks, the ordnance along the causeway, and on battery hill; our vessels immediately poured in their broadsides, and in *nine minutes* Chusan's docks, forts, and buildings were a heap of smoking ruins. Our troops landed on a deserted beach, amidst a few dead bodies, broken spears, swords, shields, and matchlocks, and moved cautiously on Ting-hai, before the strong ramparts of which they sat down for the remainder of that day. On the following morning scaling-ladders were placed against the walls, orders to mount issued, and, in a few minutes, this great city was in the possession of the invaders. This may be deemed an inglorious triumph, and military men may regret that the British had not met an enemy worthy of their prowess; but every feeling heart must unite in rejoicing at that insignificance of resistance which occasioned the less loss of life.[2] On the first of October in the following year, our fleet again returned to Chusan, to chastise the inhabitants of that island for the duplicity and falsehood of their government. Headed by the gallant Keo, and fully expecting an attack, the Chinese offered a stout resistance; but the hero and his brave staff were slain, tremendous havoc made amongst his followers, and the tragic scene that now presented itself far exceeded the desolation that attended the first capture of Ting-hai. The total inequality between the contending parties, even when Keo, a man of resolution and ability, gave an example worthy of the highest honour to his soldiers, may be judged of from the ratio of killed and wounded. On one side large numbers fell; while on the other, the British, the loss amounted to *two* killed and twenty-eight wounded.

---

[1] *Tinghai is the chief town on the island of Chusan, commanding the approaches to Hangchow.*

[2] *To give the other side of the story, the defenders rejected an offer of unconditional surrender, but had no way to retaliate against the concentrated fire of fifteen British men o'war; the military commander died of his wounds, and two high officials, the Prefect and the Chief Police Officer, committed suicide rather than surrender.*

NOWHERE, during the British descent upon the coast of China, was the destruction of life and property greater than at Ting-hai. Situated in the entrance to the bay of Hang-tchow-foo, Chusan might operate as a breakwater against the ocean's waves, a fortress against foreign wars; but in the latter capacity it proved lamentably deficient. It is remarkable that those places which the Chinese government believed to be impregnable, yielded readily to British arms, while positions of less reputation afforded more obstinate resistance. Every hill on the coast in vicinity of Ting-hai, is crowned with a battery of apparent strength; some too elevated to be effective, others too much exposed to the fire of an enemy. At the entrance of a defile, watered by a rivulet flowing from the valley of Chae-hu, and on an eminence about two hundred feet above the level of the bay, stands one of those deceptive structures, misnamed "The Fortress of Terror," in which the Chinese so lucklessly reposed entire confidence, when the British fleet cast anchor in the roads beneath.

No troops, however armed or disciplined, could have acted with more eminent personal gallantry, than the Tartar garrison of the fort of Terror, yet none ever encountered a more complete defeat. Two circumstances contributed to produce this result; one, the scientific principles, perfect discipline, and national courage of the British; the other, ignorance on the part of the Chinese, of all modern improvements in the destructive art of war. Hereafter these hill-forts may be strengthened, and rendered serviceable; yet even this hope would appear to be extinguished by the extensive application of steam in the British navy.

58
The Fortress of Terror, Ting-hai

In one of the picturesque and rocky glens of Chusan, and immediately behind the city of Ting-hai, where several spacious villas are erected, stands a strange-looking Hall of Ancestors, and, its pleasant position on an elevated rock overhanging the glen, and commanding a prospect of the fortress in front, and of the sea at its base, is a favourite place for visits. A well known paved-way, crossing an artificial river by a wooden bridge, ascends the ridge of rock on which the temple rests, and, descending on the other side, passes the lower walls of the fort, and continues to Ting-hai. Although a mandarin[1] of some consequence, as his retinue implies, is seen approaching the temple in his sedan of ceremony, the roads of Chusan were not constructed for the convenience of visitors, the gratification of travellers, or the mere objects of pleasure. Every hill is cultivated to its summits, every valley, from the mountain's foot to the river's margin; and, as industry and fertility here happily combine, a large surplus arises for the enrichment of the labourers. These harvests including rice, cotton, sweet potatoes, coarse tea, and candles made from the seeds of the tallow-tree, are conveyed along the canals in barges, and afterwards carried to the sea-ports by the usual mode of transport in China, the bamboo-pole laid across the shoulders, with buckets, or baskets, or boxes suspended from its extremities. In the agreeable scene, with which the faithful pencil of Captain Stoddart[2] has made the western world familiar, little boats are just arriving at a convenient place for landing or receiving burdens; and, beyond the pool, a picture still more animated presents itself, in the bustle of the boatmen and porters belonging to a large farm-house, the paddy grounds of which lie behind.

[1]For a definition of mandarin, see p. 11.
[2]For Captain Stoddart, see Introduction.

59
Close of the Attack on Chapoo[1]

IT was on the 17th of May, in the year 1842, that a British fleet, under the command of Vice-Admiral Sir Willam Parker,[2] arrived before the city of Chapoo; and, on the following morning, Sir Hugh Gough[3] succeeded in landing a force of 1,300 men on a sandy beach, two miles east of the city, without the least opposition from the Chinese. The enemy had assembled their entire force, 8,000 men, within the city, relying mainly on the strength of their fortifications, leaving the range of heights, a natural battery, and one that commanded their streets and the bay where the British lay, wholly unoccupied. While the British forces were ascending and forming on the hills, the ships of war opened upon the fortifications on shore, which were immediately silenced, and a brigade of 700 seamen landing, under cover of a heavy fire from the ships, drove the Chinese from their guns towards the city. Sir Hugh Gough was now in possession of the heights, from which the whole Chinese army could be seen marching through the streets, in full retreat. Their movements appeared to be hastened from time to time by the fall of shells and grape amongst them, according as the howitzers and field-pieces came nearer and nearer; at length, Colonel Schoedde's escalading party getting completely over the wall, the rapid volleys of his musketry completed the confusion and rout.

Three hundred Mantchou Tartars, feeling shamed by the desertion of so large a force, took possession of a strong building in the middle of the city, resolved to hold it against every opposition. This little devoted band had wholly escaped the notice of the pursuing army, nor was their purpose understood until they became the aggressors, by discharging a smart volley upon the rear of the Irish brigade. Some twenty of the Irish turned to revenge the injury, but they were soon obliged to retire, several of their number being instantly shot down. A second party, however, soon succeeded, and boldly advancing to the entrance, received the murderous fire of the Tartars, by which Colonel Tomlinson and several of his men fell mortally wounded.[4] British gallantry seemed to rise in proportion as danger increased, and the death of their brave companions only nerved the arms and steeled the swords of Colonel Mountain and his brave party. Assaulting the Tartar stronghold with all their national heroism, they were yet unable to gain the upper hand, and after the Colonel and his two lieutenants had been severely wounded, the attack was again abandoned. What manly daring could effect had now been accomplished by these brave Tartar soldiers, as well as by their equally gallant enemies; but military skill, scientific adjuments, and superior discipline, being at length called in, the defenders' fate was sealed. Colonel Knowles now came up with the shells and rockets, and in a few minutes the little fortress was in flames, its luckless occupants were all either shot or bayoneted, with the exception of about twenty, who were spared to grace the triumph of British military prowess.

A sort of wild despair took possession of the whole population of Chapoo, upon the sudden discovery of our infinite superiority in the art of war. The men, including 6,500 regular troops and 1,700 Tartars, abandoned the city; the women, having destroyed their children, committed suicide, and numbers were found suspended from the ceilings of their once happy homes. Amongst the spoils of Chapoo were ninety pieces of ordnance, jingalls, matchlocks, bows, and gunpowder. The loss on the part of the Chinese was estimated at 1,500 men, on ours it is known not to have exceeded nine men killed, and fifty wounded.

---

[1]Chapu, a port on the Bay of Hangchow, now superceded by Shanghai as a leading seaport.

[2]Parker took over command of the British fleet in August 1841, his appointment marking a more aggressive phase in the British operations.

[3]Gough had been in charge of the British land forces since March 1841.

[4]See illustration on p. 105.

60
Military Station at Cho-kien

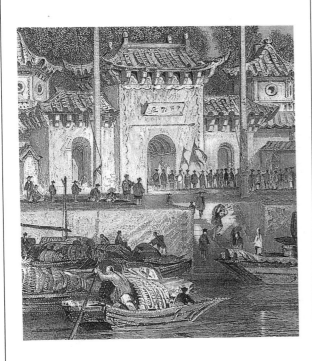

ON every navigable river, but especially on the Pei-ho, the northern feeder of the Imperial Canal, military stations are established; the magnitude or strength of each being proportioned to the population or traffic of the district. As rivers are the chief highways of China, these posts are analogous to our police-stations; and the troops lodged in them are not the regular military, but rather the local militia. Besides the maintenance of tranquillity, and enforcing the orders of government, the river-guard have other duties to perform, such as the exaction of tolls, preservation of unimpeded water-way, and care of the sluices. The accompanying view represents a station-house of the first class, where a guard of at least one hundred men is always maintained: whenever an imperial *cortège,* or the train of a mandarin of distinction, passes, it is their duty to give a military salute. This ceremony consists in the discharge of three short petards,[1] kept for this purpose alone: they are fixed perpendicularly in the ground, a little powder is first put into the barrel, over which sand and earth are tightly rammed. When the ceremony is completed, the gorgeous dresses of the soldiers, including embroidered undergarments and satin boots, together with their arms and equipment, are restored to the armoury in the station-house, and there preserved until another public occasion shall demand another distribution. As for the soldiers themselves, if they be only the Chinese military police, the greater part resume their agricultural or industrial pursuits, retaining also their pay, which is equivalent to three-pence a day of our money. This little stipend, and some additional value which attaches to office in every country, prove so attractive, that the duty of a soldier is taken, rather than put upon the people

— invitation is used to obtain, instead of conscription to enforce the service.

The military pavilion at Cho-kien is always a picturesque object, and frequently presents a scene of much bustle and animation. The vicinity of a large and navigable river, covered with a multitude of boats, and of various kinds, including junks, flower-boats, sanpans,[2] pleasure-barges, chop-boats,[3] and others, must necessarily present an endless variety of scene and incident. Here are continued arrivals and departures, frequent disputes between the junkmen and pullers and occasional punishments of criminals from the surrounding country; for, although the imperial power is so overwhelming, that neighbouring states can offer to it no serious resistance, amongst the Chinese themselves, and in the very heart of the empire, convulsions, insurrections, conspiracies, and tumults, are of hourly occurrence, and give ample employment to the standing police and the regular Tartar soldiers. In front of the pavilion are hoisted the national flags, yellow, white, red, and blue, or one of these colours bordered with the other if the garrison consist entirely of Tartar troops; but, green banners with red borders, or the reverse, in the centre of which is displayed the national gilt dragon, if of Chinese.

---

[1] *A kind of small explosive weapon used for forcing gates, etc.*

[2] *Sampan: a small, nondescript craft in general use, equivalent to an English rowing boat.*

[3] *Large vessels for use on creeks and inner waterways, moved by poles, for carrying foreign personnel from point to point; so-called because they carried papers with official seal (chop), authorising their business.*

THE OPIUM WAR (1839–1842)

The war began unofficially on 4 September 1839 when a fleet of Chinese warjunks, bent on preventing the British from receiving local food supplies, clashed with British warships off Kowloon. This was followed by a similar clash two months later off Chuenpi. The British Indian Government, on behalf of the British Crown, issued a formal declaration of war to the Chinese Empire on 31 January, three weeks after an imperial decree from Peking had banned British trade from China 'for ever'. In the meantime Palmerston, acting without consulting Parliament, was already organizing a force to go to China.

The actual conduct of the war falls into three parts, namely the operations in the Pearl River Estuary and around Canton, and the two British naval expeditions up the China Coast. The operations in the Pearl River were handled by the acting Superintendent of (British) Trade, Captain Charles Elliott. At first, action was confined to occasional naval clashes and the bombardment of the Chinese forts guarding the approaches of the river. From June 1840, when the first British naval force arrived, Canton was put under British blockade but no real attempt was made to invest the city until early the following year when the breakdown of the Tientsin truce (see below) led to an attack on the key forts in the Bocca Tigris, on Chuenpi and Taikoktow islands. The success of these attacks led Ki-shen, the senior Chinese official at Canton, to sign the Convention of Chuenpi with Charles Elliott on 20 January 1841, which incidentally provided for the cession of Hong Kong to the British. However, the Convention was immediately denounced by London as gaining too little and by Peking as giving away too much, and both Elliott and Ki-shen faced dismissal and disgrace. The war resumed and a British force moved up to Canton, destroying all the Chinese river forts on the way, and would have easily taken the city had the Cantonese not opted for a ransom to save themselves. So the British withdrew. This was Elliott's last act, for he was now replaced by his successor, Sir Henry Pottinger.

However, the main thrust of the British campaign was a naval one. It was quite clear that no amount of pressure at Canton would make the Chinese see British reason. By June 1840, a naval force under the command of Rear-Admiral George Elliott, the cousin of Charles, had assembled off Macao, and at the end of that month, with the two Elliotts on board, it sailed northwards to Tientsin, bombarding and burning on the way. The arrival of this fleet at Tientsin, too close to the capital for comfort, was sufficient for Ki-shen, newly-appointed to replace the disgraced opium-destroying Imperial Commissioner, Lin Tse-hsu, to negotiate a truce (at Tientsin in October 1840) and persuade the Elliotts to conclude the negotiations at Canton. It was the breakdown of these negotiations at Canton (through no fault of Ki-shen's) which led to the attack on the Bogue forts and the Convention of Chuenpi already mentioned.

The final stage was the second naval expedition up the China coast led by Admiral Parker and Sir Henry Pottinger. This reinforced and much more powerful fleet left Macao in August 1841 and, having reduced a number of places on the way, captured Ningpo (in October) which became the British base for the winter. After repulsing a Chinese counterattack the following March (1842), the British entered the Yangtze, taking Woosung, Shanghai, and against stiffening opposition, the key port of Chingkiang. By the beginning of August they were at the gates of Nanking. The British force now posed a real threat to Peking's food supplies from the Yangtze basin, and under this stimulus a new Imperial Commissioner, Ki-ying, hastened southwards to treat with the enemy. The result was, after only three weeks of negotiation, the Treaty of Nanking (signed on 29 August 1842) which brought the war to an end.

China Opium Smokers.

Glossary of Chinese Place Names

The idiosyncratic spelling of Wright and Allom in the text has been rendered here into the more familiar system developed by Wade and Giles. This system was the preferred system up until 1949. However all Chinese names now follow the official *pinyin* system. The principal places mentioned in the text are listed below in the three variants.

TEXT	WADE-GILES	PINYIN	TEXT	WADE-GILES	PINYIN
Amoy	Amoy [Hsia-men]	Xiamen	Quang-tchou	Ch'uanchow [Ch'uan-chou]	Quanzhou
Bocca Tigris (The Bogue)	Hu-mên	Humen	Shanghai	Shanghai	Shanghai
			Saipoo	Hsia-p'u	Xiapu
Canton	Canton [Kuang-chou]	Guangzhou	Soo-chow-foo	Hsüchow [Hsü-chou]	Xuzhou
Chapoo	Cha-p'u	Zhapu	Tcharing (Lake)	Tsaring Nor (or Cha-ling Hu)	Zhaling Hu
Chin-hai	Chen-hai	Zhenhai	Tien-sing	Tientsin [T'ien-chin]	Tianjin
Ching-keang-foo	Chinkiang [Chin-chiang]	Zhenjiang	Ting-hai	Tinghai	Dinghai
Chuenpee	Chuenpi (or Ch'uan-pi)	Chuanbi	Tong-chow-foo	T'ungchow [T'ung-chou]	Tongzhou
Chusan (Island)	Chusan [Chou-shan]	Zhoushan			*[Tongxian]
Hang-tchow-foo	Hangchow [Hang-chou]	Hangzhou	Tsuen-tcheou-foo	Changchow (or Chang-chou)	Zhangzhou
Heong-keong	Hong Kong [Hsiang-kang]	Xianggang	Tycocktow	Taikoktow (or Ta-chiao-t'ou)	Dajiaotou
Hoang-ho (River)	Huang-ho	Huanghe	Whampoa	Whampoa (or Huang-p'u)	Huangpu
Hong-tse (Lake)	Hung-tze (Hu)	Hongze (Hu)	Woo-sung	Wusung	Wusong
King-tan (Kiangsu Prov.)	Chin-t'an	Jintan	Yang-tcheou	Yangchow [Yang-chou]	Yangzhou
			Yang-tse-kiang (River)	Yangtze Kiang [Yang-tzu Chiang]	Yangzijiang *[Changjiang]
Kokonor (Lake)	Tsinghai (Hu)	Qinghai (Hu)	Yao (River)	Yao	Yao
Lea-ou-tong	Liaotung	Liaodong	Yellow River (See Hoang Ho)		
Nanking	Nanking [Nan-ching]	Nanjing	Zhehol	Jehol (or Ch'engtê)	Chengde
Nine-bend River (English)	Chiu-lung Kiang [Chiu-lung Chiang]	Jiulongjiang			
Ningpo	Ningpo	Ningbo			
Oring (Lake)	Oring Nor (or O-ling Hu)	Eling Hu			
Pei Ho (River)	Pei-yün Ho	Beiyunhe			
Peking	Peking [Pei-ching]	Beijing			
Quang-choo-foo	Canton [Kuang-chou]	Guangzhou			

*the common form in today's maps

[Those in square brackets in the Wade-Giles column are the correct form according to the Wade-Giles system, but most of them are in less common usage.]

Note: FOO (*pinyin*, FU) is a term for an administrative district (often rendered as prefecture): used as suffix for many place names.
CHOW (Wade-Giles, CHOU; *pinyin*, ZHOU): terms for administrative district smaller than FU: also used as a suffix.

THE EIGHTEEN PROVINCES OF CHINA PROPER

WADE-GILES	PINYIN
Anhwei	Anhui
Chekiang	Zhejiang
Chihli (Hopeh)	Hebei
Fukien	Fujian
Honan	Henan
Hunan	Hunan
Hupeh	Hubei
Kansu	Gansu
Kiangsi	Jiangxi
Kiangsu	Jiangsu
Kwangsi	Guangxi
Kwangtung	Guangdong
Kweichow	Guizhou
Shansi	Shanxi
Shantung	Shandong
Shensi	Shaanxi
Szechuan	Sichuan
Yunnan	Yunnan